T0103445

YOURS...
EVEN THOUGH YOU
ARE NOT MINE

YOURS...
EVEN THOUGH YOU ARE NOT MINE

MUKESH PANDEY

PARTRIDGE
A Penguin Random House Company

ISBN: Softcover   978-1-4828-4983-7
               eBook   978-1-4828-4982-0

Print information available on the last page.

To order additional copies of this book, contact
Partridge India
000 800 10062 62
orders.india@partridgepublishing.com

www.partridgepublishing.com/india

Dedicated to

The loving memory of the girl I
loved, yet could not marry...
You'll always be more than just a story in my life...

ACT ONE

When It All Started...

Navi Mumbai

It was Mid-April. Summer was at its peak. Usually every college in Mumbai had farewell party for the seniors. So did our college...

So as it was farewell celebration in our school, we were supposed to reach at the venue before the seniors. The venue was our college itself. So that we can arrange all the stuff such as snacks, soft drinks a bit of a light dinner and of course the entertainment that includes dance-drama-singing or whatever we can do to make our seniors happy. After all they are going to leave the school for god's sake and leave us alone as well... in my second thought I used to think farewell parties were just a bribe the school used to give their students to let them know that even thou we fucked your childhood with the worst teachers and subjects, even if they didn't have the best quality of studies to offer us they still want you to announce that "OUR COLLEGE WAS THE BEST!!" when you leave their campus and get admission in another campus..

Our college was a well known college in Navi Mumbai. It was formally known as "Tilak Junior College"

Well, it was another morning for me. I was in no hurry again. Life was awesome I did not have to worry about the early morning lectures, shouting professors or pending homework, So for the day I woke up at 11, we were supposed to reach there at 4:00 PM. I got ready in the best possible clothes in my wardrobe... I wore a red T-Shirt with black strips on it & a black trouser... I was not really found of jeans those days with a black leather shoe! Of course a pair of socks beneath it... all and all looked well enough to attend a farewell party.

That day my friend Naresh came to pick me up. He was the only guy in our class who had a bike a Bajaj Boxer... He was a nice guy 6ft 2inch tall & a gold chain in his neck the gold rings in his hands there were total of 5 in both the hands and why not his dad has 2 jewelry shops in Mumbai, he was a rich guy. He picked me up at 3:00 PM.....

'Where we are going first?" I asked while jumping on his bike's back seat,

"We are going to get married at the Bandra court you idiot" he said looking at me and kicked started his bike we both burst into laughter. On our way I teased him as if he is my wife and I hold him tight from back, and said "u don't drive well darling would you mind if your husband drive" and I laughed at my own joke "kiss my ass u jerk" he said irritated..

"Where are the guys" I asked shocked as I if have forgotten to wear my pants...

"Oh they! They reached there and called me up to pick you & be there on time don't worry" he said calmly.

We reached at our destination in 10 minutes. He stopped the bike at the main gate of our college I get down there, and he went ahead to the parking area to park his bike. I stood at the gate watching all the girls of our batch dressed well in Indian dresses we all knew each other very well I talked to some girls as I was very good in cracking conversation with girls..

"Oh you looking pretty" I said with a wink to a girl in our batch

"Ya I always doo look the same" Heena said quite arrogantly...

"Is that a fake smile on your face?" I asked

"No, why would I fake a smile" she said shocked with my comment

"Ya I knew it you are damn happy to see me" again with a wink... and a naughty smile the add-on

"You'll never change, come inside everybody is waiting" she smiled and said waving her hand in the gesture to follow her.

In the meanwhile Naresh came "sorry bro! The parking area was full so have to found some another space to park my bike" he said disgracefully "how could all the bastards in our class got bike's" I said in his reply of no space in the parking lot..

"Maybe they'd have rubbed their asses to get it from their dad" he countered sternly "dumb asses" I shouted and we moved in..

It was well decorated our college managed to do some good work at last, finally the stage the buffet system the stereo system the chairs they were kept in the perfect order.. Some geek students of our batch were already sitting on the first row.. "It's not an examination hall or a quiz contest" I wondered why they loved sitting on the first row even in our class those were the faces that could be easy visible on the first row... 'Book insects' I thought in my mind and moved away from there..

"Hey Maddy" I heard a voice shouting at me, I turned my back even Naresh turned along and we saw Raj waving his hands in air as if he has came at the airport to receive us..

"There they are" Naresh said and moved ahead towards him...

"What's up brother" raj said and we hugged each other, "This could have been your farewell my brother" I said just to tease him.

"Why not you asshole!!" he replied disgustedly Naresh and I went into a huge laugh...

Raj was our senior in the last year and senior of my seniors' before that, so practically it was his third Farwell party! Poor guy..

"Where are Shrikant, Peter and Venket" Naresh asked raj, snatching the Maaza from his hand

"Hey you can get another one from the food area, give me back my Maaza" raj shouted and managed to snatch his Maaza back.

"Ohh the Stud is here" peter said coming towards me hugged me and punched me as he was doing it from past 5-6 years... Peter was probably the 2nd fattest guy in our school after Saad one my senior or u can say Raj's old friend... Shrikant kept smiling he was not the guy who use to laugh or talk a lot I wonder how we became such good friends as he was one of the top rankers not in our batch but in our college as well.,

"Naa Naa, the stud is there itself" I pointed towards the stage .. Peter, Naresh, & raj they leaned towards the wall to see whom I was pointing...

"Ahh, the blackboard" Naresh said (Blackboard= Venket) he was a Tamilian and most of them have dark complexion, they all saw him and without saying a word we moved towards the stage where our stud was having a conversation with one of our professor Hegde Sir!

Hegde sir was our Sports teacher; the reason Venket was his favorite because of his sports skills. And yes the Tamilian was a great sportsman getting two back to back sportsmen of the year award. But this year I was one of his hardest competitor.. At least I hope so.

Maybe this was the reason he was buttering our sports teacher? Aahhmmm..

But we were very good friends first and competitors later...

"Hey partner" I said and patted back on Venket's shoulder, while Hegde sir looked me as if I have interrupted him during the rapid fire round and he was about to win a gift hamper'

"Hey jerk you came" said our smiling Tamilian and we hugged each other so do the other guys did; we greeted Hegde sir as he left as alone...

"So at what time will the party start" I asked Venket looking at my wristwatch

He said yawning "let the senior's come first" I knew poor guy was bored with the conversation with our very own 'Harsha Bhogle" of our college... Mr.Hegde, I still don't what was his first name as everyone in the college use call him that itself.,

It was 7:00 pm and the entire senior's where made seated to the chairs which were kept nicely facing towards the stage and all the geek students who were at the first row has moved there way for the Principal-Vice. Principle and the all other staff members...

As the celebration progressed it felt great we had great fun as expected it was dance drama and singing and a bit of book reading form one of our very talented 'GEEK' Aazam I mean how could he managed to carry a book with him to a party venue.. It was a bouncer to me..

As the party headed towards the end there were some prize distribution to be made, the best Dancer which went to Arya for his great Bharatnatyam skills.. And many more prizes.

And then it came to the "BEST STUDENT OF THE YEAR" yes you read it right it was given every year to the student who has managed Great studying skills and good behavior in the college with the staff member and with the student as well.,

Our class teacher Pushpa Miss was the anchor that evening she was one of those teacher who I think use to take out all his grudges with student because she had a fight with his husband every morning, don't know? Maybe? I guess??

And then she began the announcement first he played with everybody's emotion saying "Any guesses?" "Any guesses" there were only two name which everyone shouted one it was Nitin Desai and second was Durgesh Pandey,

And then she broke the suspense and announced "The student of the year goes to none another than Durgesh pandey" and she had a glass of water and the clapped surrounded my ear all around the stage and the school., the guy stood and went up the stage to collect the trophy from our principle MR.Kurup. He acknowledged everyone's claps. And stood there on the stage

And that's when Pushpa miss shot the bullet in my head, I mean not actually, but sort of.

Yes she used to look like a "bandit queen"...

She said "So what to do you think guys was he deserving" everyone clapped harder to prove that yes he was dam deserving guy... And some of his friends screamed "undoubtedly" "200 percent" and claps were still on, "ok wait now calm down everyone" she said showing her right hand to the students as 'goddess laxmi'

"So who deserve the Worst student of the year" and she smiled cunningly looking at me.. I knew she has shot the bullet and she said again "I think it should be brother of Durgesh isn't it Durgesh" she looked at Durgesh and he also nodded his head. 'Fuck' I said,

YES DURGESH IS MY ELDER BROTHER! Still there wasn't any such trophy or award to be given to the "worst student of the year" but her saying was all enough... The crowd started hooting and clapping, for one second

7

I thought as if I have won the Oscars award for the best actor?? Naa I couldn't be luckier than 'Leonardo Di Caprio' we both had a similar story... Neither he won an Oscar and not even me.

"Even thou I have attended three farewell, this one is the best" raj said laughing and trying to control his laugh after noticing my anger. But friends are friends they kept hooting and shouting as if seriously I have to walk towards the stage and collect some memento, if there would be one I had to reach there it would have called as 'Walk of the guilt' I felt like killing my teacher but still managed to standup smile and wave my hands like "**mujhe apna vote zaroor dijiyega**"

The party ended on that note all the teachers and professors were busy giving the entire senior's tip for their bright future and suggesting them the best college in Mumbai.

We all junior were out of the gate, Raj, Venket, Shrikant, Peter they all called an auto and went for dinner I said I won't be coming because I was sleepy, Naresh was also suppose to join them but I convinced him to drop me home and then join them 'he agreed.. He came on his Bajaj Boxer to gate and said "common dude am hungry let me thro u at your place and then drive again to the group" I was about to take the back seat of the bike the... I heard a female voice saying..

"Hey Maddy You Going??"

"Hey Shatabdi, where were you all thru the party" Naresh said looking towards her

"I was busy laughing, that's a big compliment buddy" she said looking towards me maybe? and couldn't control her laughter, I heard her giggles it went like someone had played my favorite music in my earphone in loud volume but on the other hand I knew she was pointing that 'Worst Student Of The Year' topic I didn't looked at her and kept my head down..

But finally I managed to look at her face ... And then what I saw was something that made my Life... <3

ACT TWO

Shatabdi

I was looking at her, her eyes had something to say, a passionate desire. Strikingly beautiful – she was. The soft drizzle rendered her even more beautiful. Lips wet and her clothes drenched kissing her body elucidating her ravishing figure. The curls outlining her face proved to be slide to the sizzle. My eyes were wide open as if I had just seen god. Actually, I had. Not God, rather a Goddess. A Goddess, whose flawless beauty was untouched and undiscovered by this world,

Adjectives, I was short of. Diva- Hottie- Sexy- Ravishing- were words quite insufficient to describe even a bit of her Beauty. I was lost as if in am another world. Her presence had captured me and flushed my mind of all of its lust-less thoughts.

Some distance away from her, I stood. Completely lost, in her dream. It was the first time I found her true beauty, even thou we are very good friends.

Shatabdi Biswas- the best girl I have ever seen.. I mean she is been my classmate from past 4years, we have been very good friends.. but Today it was something different about her don't know why but I felt like I was In a different world, I was lost in her eyes those eyes has such depth, I knew I have hit by an invisible disease called 'LOVE <3'

"what happen, why you looking at me like that" she said so sweetly I only managed to say was "how come Tajmahal pays visit to our school, is it for the party Begum sahiba?" I flirted but this time I was In love, I couldn't manage to move my eyes from her

"That was cheesy" she said moving her lips towards left and smiling too.

"if that's cheesy would u like to be a rat and eat that cheese now itself" I said she laughed loudly and moved her hands towards me to give a high-five..

I was happy that I made her smile.. I was patting my back when a sound hit my ears again but this time it was irritating,

"Bhai chalna nai hai kya?" Naresh said me while he was been a spectator for a while...

"Ya yaw u guys carry on even I'll leave now" Shatabdi said looking at her wrist watch and waved her hands like a kid to say "Bye"

"How will u be going? It's almost 10:30" I said reminding her that it's quiet late,

"I'll take a rickshaw from the rickshaw stand" she said casually pointing towards the rickshaw stand which was just beside the main gate of our college,

"Ok ok, I'll walk with you till there" I said and started walking with her she waved her hand towards Naresh...

"bro should I leave?" Naresh said as he was quite pissed off and hungry to...

"U can leave brother u need to join them" I said instantly as I wanted him to leave as soon as he can so I can spend some alone time with Shatabdi even if it's for 5minutes. "Fuck you bastard" he said me & said "bye" to Shatabdi" and pulled the accelerator of bike as if he is he is pulling my ears if he gets a chance, and got vanished in seconds before I could say anything..

"So now how you'll go home?" Shatabdi asked as we walked towards the rickshaw stand "probably even I'll take a rickshaw" and winked, and hoped she under stand's that I left a fully paid trip towards my home just to be with her for five minutes,

"Bhaiyya Vashi Sector-15 chaloge" she asked to the first rickshaw waala in the line, "haan madam challenge naa, baithiye" he said adjusting his spectacles and leaning towards the kick of rickshaw to pull it..

She sat inside the rickshaw "Bye sambhal ke jaana take care" for me it was like 'nothing should happen to you are mine' I was dreaming with my eyes wide open.. "Bye you take care, & do have your dinner once you reach home" I said I got seated in the rickshaw next in the line "KoperKhairne station" I said and I went home.

All that night I was thinking about that last 5 minutes with her.. They were fantastic... I wanted to meet her again soon..

ACT THREE

The Best Buddies

It's was almost a week after the farewell party I was having my lunch at home, my cell phone beeped one time and I knew it's a message! I always kept my phone at vibration mode at my place just to avoid or create scene at home my dad was a very strict father we rarely talked to each other, my brother the "Student Of The Year" he had an easy going with my father and my family members, I was not like him at all.,

I mostly use to spend my days at college ground playing cricket after all I wanted to beat Venket for the 1st time and be the "sportsmen of the year" and during my lectures all that happens was professors and teachers yelling at me for the same reason of course "why don't you study" "cricket will not shape up your future" "why don't you learn something from your brother" I mostly use to have nap during the lectures or don't attend it for ages but when I use to return to class sometimes I even heard from guys **"who is he?" "never seen him in the class?"** and when I attend lectures next me use to sit 'RAJ' yes the man himself who knew nothing about studies all he knew was our English teacher Laxmi miss was hot! And he was dam right about it..

But as now I wanted to be with Shatabdi all the time I use to attend every lectures which included her, some of my friends started saying me "dude are you ok" I said confusingly "yaw! Why?" "naa naa you are regular in the class nowadays so we thought there something's wrong" and they laughed, obviously it was that students who's faces was what I got to see when I enter the class in the morning, I use to think maybe they get dressed up for the lectures one day before the lectures.. 'Dumbasses' ...

My friendship with Shatabdi was getting better and better day by day, but I didn't had the courage to let her know that am madly in love with her, apart from her every one of my batch got to know that "yes this guy is mad about that girl,."

We use to sit together, walk together, eat together, and studies yes I use to be with her during the studies but, it was something like couldn't do it., imagine even the girl I was In love with was not able to make me study., that's how much I hated studies but for her I started compromising with everything just to be with her., I use to keep my book open and sit in front of her and she u to say "Reading naa?" I use to nod my head like a obedient child I loved her each and everything the way she use to say "naa?" after every sentence I felt like 'girl you are making me fall for you over and over again"

2 years passed by and our friendship was rock solid till now I always wanted to be her best friend first, so that if she doesn't like me being her partner she doesn't breaks the friendship, another reason was making her believe that we both needed each other and I was very much succeeded in that we both were so much connected till now that no one of us could have broken the friendship for any reason,.

It was our last exam that day. The exams went well. Like incredibly well. There was an outside chance that I might even score higher than her, but then, even if I did, the entire credit would go to Shatabdi for she made me work hard as I had, I had a plan that after our final exam I'll ask her out and then I'll propose her... All was going good, the day came I was waiting at the main gate of our college to let her come...

And there she came my girl? Not yet! But soon to be...

"Hey Shattu, how your exams went" I asked her in a relaxed way stretching my arms and yawning, In the past few years we were such good buddies I gave her few pet names as well 'Shattu' was one of it...

"Awesome" she said with a smile and hugged her books... I wanted to be that book at that time no matter how much I hated studies I could have been a book just to get a hug from her... and her smiles just kills me and make me fall for her all over again.. She was looking as beautiful as always she was wearing a blue top & a brown full length skirt.,

"So what's the plan now" I asked taking the first step to execute my plan.

"Nothing much, going at Pinky's place then will be going together at my place for lunch" she said obviously she didn't know what's on my mind and pinky is her cousin she looked like 'Kiran Bedi' the former IPS,.

"Ohh I have nothing to do getting bored" I fired a bullet just to get her sympathy

"where are the other guys" she said completely ignoring as if I was a beggar and was asking for a 10 rupee note?,

"Ahh., they... th... thheeyy.. Went home u know how they are" I told her breathing heavily and lying to her, if my friends would have got to know this they would have killed me there itself,

"kitne kamine hai sab ke sab naa?, now what you'll do here go home take some rest" she said and again that 'naa' this line reminded me of saying in a bollywood movie **'ladki kaa naa matlab haan"**

I have waited for this day from past 2 years I couldn't let it slip away from me I said to myself, she was waiting for my reply as I was standing in front of her! Blocking her way? Not really...

I said "toh, you are going by rickshaw" that was a silly question but I needed the conversation to get going..

"Obviously, I don't have a car naa baba" she said like a kid tilting her head towards left... I didn't knew what to say next yes I was very good to crack a conversation with the other girls but this girl was special! DAMM SPECIAL!! Still I managed to say something that I was proud of..

"chalke jaate hai? Even am going vashi for work will talk about it in between what say?" I said and wished form bottom of my heart that she says yes..

"kya kaam hai vashi mein tumhein?" she said remarking my last sentence

"Nothing big I need to go to raj's place" Raj the outmost senior of my batch luckily he use to stay where Shatabdi lived, even thou he was still in the examination hall I wanted to visit him at his place? But who cares!

"Chalke?" she said her eyes wide open as if I have asked her to swim thru the Arabian ocean and come back,

"Haan what's the big deal chalo natak mat karo" I said ordering her as we were "BEST BUDDIES" till now I can say those things easily to her..

"OK" she said like an obedient child and my plan had worked till now...

And we started our walk.

"Walk a bit slower, my legs aren't long as yours" she said standing at one place her both hands on her waist and eyes slightly open trying to avoid the sun...

"Oh sorry! Come.. Come will walk together now" I said holding my ears and smiling, waiting for her to forgive me. "That's ok baba!" she said hitting on my hands in which I was holding my ears...

'Now is the time come on dude you have to tell her how you feel for her' I was talking to myself.. "What happen, is everything ok" she said looking at me..

"Ya all good," I said and continued again "Not actually" ... "kya hogaya" she replied...

"See I wanted to say you something form many days I couldn't gather enough courage to talk to you regarding it" I said and then realized now I can't back off I have to say it..

"It's like. . . . ." I was about to say it but she interrupted me in between and said "Look Maddy I know what you want to say to me" she said looking down on the road as if she has lost a 2rupee coin...

Meanwhile I was shocked.. And surprised.. But it was obvious she would know that I was found of her.. The whole college knew about it so does she.. I only managed to say was "So do you also love . . . .

"And again she interrupted me in between and said "yes I love you but as a friend, we can't be life partner we aren't made for each other" she said and tried not looking into my eyes...

She said it... I stand stood near a cake shop "Ribbons And Balloons" next to next her building.. All I wanted to hear from her was only the starting three words she said, it wasn't like that.. She didn't loved me and she said it.. It was nothing I could have said to her it was me, myself who was trying to be her best friend from past 2 years... and now all that I could manage was only to be her *'Friend..'*

"Am Sorry" she said and went walking inside her compound... I didn't say a word to her...

Girls have no idea how much it hurts when our love is rejected, yet men are expected to keep trying and take hits all the time.

ACT FOUR

Falling In Love

Almost a year passed by from that day, I didn't had a word with her, and not even she tried to do so, I kept a safe distance from her I don't wanted to face her, because I couldn't, the all courage I had I gathered it to talk her about my feelings, I didn't have more courage to talk to her again about It, if I do so she would again cut my sentence in between and register myself as her "lifelong friend" and I didn't wanted to be in her 'friend zone' so I stayed away from her. I attended every class and sat in the front row. I took notes like a stenographer. I never asked the professor any questions. I even ignored all of my friends in the class as if they were from another planet or having a non curable disease.

I didn't knew what to do I even convinced my elder sister Poonam didi that I'll be shifting to my native place for the further studies or I'll look for a job over there., she was confused and said "Tu pehle aa yahan fir dekhte hai" and I was ready to leave I got my tickets' to Lucknow form Kurla terminus the train was on 14th April..

It was 12th April when I got a call from peter "hello" I said after pressing the green button on my cell phone. "Where the fuck you are, you rascal why aren't you picking up my call from so many days, you moron….." he continued as he was very angry on me as I didn't received his call from past one month I interrupted him and said "bro am leaving on 14th"

"What the fuck, where are you going now?" he said in his loud voice.

"Am leaving Mumbai, m going to sister's place my ticket is been done I'll leave at 9pm on 14th" I said and kept quiet and waited for him to burst on me.

"Is this because Shatabdi said she don't love you right?" he said in a very calm voice... I was surprised I said "did you had a word with her? What did she said?" my excitement was obvious. "Dude meet me tomorrow I need to talk to you, and am calling Shatabdi as well" he said and disconnected the call.

13th APRIL

That day morning I got a call from peter at 11AM he said me to come near the KoperKhairne stations ticket counter he was waiting there for me along with Raj, Shatabdi and her 4 year old cousin Shudeep.

In next few minutes I was there I met every one and said hi to Shatabdi as well.

"What's wrong with you Maddy?" Shatabdi said after I greeted her with a 'hi'... I didn't knew what happened for a second and she continued "why are you leaving Mumbai? Is this because of me" I knew peter told her about my departure from Mumbai and my behavior with them.

"paagal hai kya? Why would you be reason" I said smiling and trying to hide my pain of getting rejected by her. "accha.. toh fir…." She said folding her hands across but peter interrupted her and said "am hungry, pehle kuch khaa le" looking at his size anyone would say he is hungry 24X7. "Oh yes even am dam hungry" Raj said and went to start his bike.. Shatabdi was still looking at me fiercely as a tigress watching her prey to come near to attack.

I looked in her eyes I couldn't manage to look at for more than 2seconds.

We went to 'Shubhlaxmi' a restaurant near to KoperKhairne station we all had something where Shudeep had ice-creams and chocolates which I bought for him while everyone was busy having what they ordered.

We finished everything I paid the bill and came out of the restaurant.

Just when we came out of the restaurant, peter said me he needs to talk to Shatabdi regarding me; I didn't interrupted him in that. Peter Shatabdi & her cousin went walking towards the station, while I and raj also followed them slowly.

"Don't worry brother" raj said with a cunning smile on his face, "worry?? about what?" I said looking at him. "Arey Bhai, we all know we are here for you and Shatabdi" he said and kept his right hand on my shoulder, I didn't said any word and kept walking...

"There they are" raj said pointing peter and Shatabdi standing far from us near the parking area,

We walked to them "hey Shatabdi wants to talk to you" peter came near me and whispered in my ear, and winked me... I didn't understood what he was trying to say. but I knew that something good is going to happen. Shatabdi was standing near my bike and his younger cousin was sitting on it as if he is going to drop us home. I walked towards Shatabdi.

There was something in her eyes that day, actually it was me.. I was looking myself in her eyes.. I was happy at least I have managed to be in her eyes., but I wanted to be in her heart for forever..

She came near me and said "I LOVE YOU TOO" I was shaken, shocked.. And confused altogether. For few minutes I didn't realize what she said.. "Whatt,?" I said with my eyes wide open… and dying to hear that again from her.. "I Love You Idiot," she said again and gave a big smile..

"okay," I said and moved my hand inside my jeans to find the keys of my bike. "what ok,? I said I love you and you are not even responding to it" she said I could clearly see her eyes turning red as she was angry.

"come 'on peter convinced you to tell me that so I don't leave Mumbai, isn't it, ab mazaak band kare" I said in an irritated way, all I thought that when peter told me he needs to talk to Shatabdi he made a plan with her and she is just helping him in that plan so I stay here.

"Arey stupid, I'll punch your face, don't you get it I love you., I swear on Shudeep" she said and kept his right hand on Shudeep's head as if she is giving blessings to him. "But why?" I asked my question was meaningless but I wanted to know why she began to love me in just last 1 hour when she came in morning she was quite pissed off with me..

"It's like now I know you really love me" she said and kept her head down and hands till on Shudeep head and she continued "Peter told me how much you love me and what you feel for me exactly, there are many guys who says they love a girl but they fail to prove, and I know you won't let me down I trust you, you are my best friend I know you so well you can't cheat me, trust me am saying this not because peter told me to do so, he just made me believe in your love,

I love you, I really do" she said we both kept quiet for some time., I was in shocked and so happy that I was out of words and probably she was waiting for me to say something..

I moved my hands towards her hands and hold her hand; when I held them I was sure am going to hold it forever.

I didn't say a word and held her in my Arms. I wish I had a button to pause that moment at that very second, I can still feel that hug, Her Hug said it all... <3., Sometimes you meet someone, and it's so clear that two of you, on some level belong to each other.

Suddenly I felt all my broken pieces came together with that hug, suddenly I got a strong reasons to live my life at my fullest, suddenly everything in this world felt so beautiful, suddenly Just suddenly...

"Sometimes you can't explain what you see in a person, it's just the way they take you to a place where no one else can"

ACT FIVE

In Her Arms

"No am canceling my ticket, I want to spend some time with you," I said on the phone lying in my bed,

"Are you gone mad, u have your tickets, and if you cancel it dads going to be very angry, am not saying you to be there just as your usual tour you should visit didi's place" she said consoling me..

As we were friends first from past 5 years she knew everyone in my house and I knew her she was even a good friend of my brother as we all were in the same college,

Somehow she convinced me to go, and I left Mumbai for one month to visited my native place and my elder sister's house, even Shatabdi went Kolkata for a relative's marriage.

During those periods we use to talk hours on phone we were not worried of STD bills thanks to reliance communication they use to provide a service called 'Reliance to Reliance free" and we use to make the most of it...

That one month was like 1 century for us, but that one month broke the ice and we both realized that we both need each other like anything, even thou it was just the beginning of our LOVE...

We were back in Mumbai after a one month of vacation's... I reached at 11:30 AM in the morning, and she at 3:00 PM in the evening same day...

We both decided to meet today itself... We were suppose to meet at 6 pm at Vashi station,

I left my place at 4 pm I visited some gift shops to get something for her...as it was our official first date and I wanted to leave an impression although she knew the kind of a guy I was., when unable to find something good for her at the gift shop I decided to give her a 13Red Roses. As 13th was the day when we officially went from single to couple.

It was 8:30 when she came, a rickshaw stopped and she got down, slowing moving towards me I could see her slightly visible and then she was clearly visible to me... Beautiful face, black eyes, curved shaped eyelashes, eyebrows shaped like bow, giving perfect contrast to her complexion. Chocolate color lip gloss on her pink lips, her lips were like pulp of a flower, her untied hair fell on her cheeks with a gust of wind, she was wearing blue colored salwar kameez, matching blue earrings that hypnotized me for a moment, red cheeks, a cute face.

She looked like a baby girl. But I looked at her as my soul-mate; her body appeared so perfect, so young, so poised... Combo pack Baby and Babe, I smiled...

I wanted to look at her from top to bottom, very slowly, I did so. She looked at me; I turned my sight and then body to the other side. Anxious, shivering, my heart beats ran with horses. I tried to behave as if I was relaxed and cool but reality was inside my heart, I was nervous. She smiled that tired to override my senses. Silence between us made me more nervous. We didn't talk much and exited the station...

"She isn't only cute but hot also" my mind punched on my heart.

"Maddy! Shut up, she is your love, don't think all these rubbish things" looking downwards in shame, I ignored.

I planned many things, first I'll shake hands then a proper smile and then we will talk and I'll ask her few questions but nothing happened.

She asked, glances to the left during speech, "What happened?"

I synchronized my steps with her, went ahead a bit, and said "Nothing"

She seemed shy and silent. Obviously, her state of mind wasn't different from mine. On phone, we talked for hours and hours per day but form last thirty minutes we hardly talked for more than ten minutes. We reached CCD. We were trying to ignore to look into each other's eyes. I wanted to tell her many things but... how, that was the question. She picked up the menu. I got the best time to look at her when she was looking at the menu, though I couldn't see her face but I could feel her. I wanted to stop the watch.

Suddenly she asked, looking at me, "what do you want?"

I just turned my eyes to the other side. I was sure she understood that I was looking at her from past few minutes.

I looked into her eyes for a while. So beautiful and they said many things, there was something special in them.

"Whatever you like, you can order," I replied, turned my eyes and again looked into her eyes.

"Okay I'll order, one brownie and two cappuccino" she grinned.

"Okay" I grinned too.

'Why didn't she order only one coffee, so that I could have a sip on the same place where she touched her lips?' I Imagined.

We took time to get comfortable and then started talking. After having few sips of coffee, I said

"You are looking beautiful" and gave her those 13 roses I got for her, she was very happy to see those rose more than what I expected. I dropped her at her place around 9:00 pm and went my place, that night we talked till 4 AM until she slept while the call was not disconnected... "Hello hello, you slept?" I said voice barely escaping my throat as I didn't wanted to wakeup anyone, I said again "I think you have slept just want you to remind I love u a lot" and as I was about to disconnect the call she murmured "*I Love you to babu*" I didn't said a word just gave her a kiss thru the phone it was so passionate kiss even Dhirubhai Ambani could have felt saliva.

As Everyone Says Time Flows Away, It Flew In Our Case As Well...
7 Years Later...

People say that love is pure, love is blind, love is fair, love is unfair, love enhances oneself or love spoils oneself, but I haven't experienced anything. My feelings have not been changed nor am I. I am still the same guy who cries watching any romantic movie, who abuses the Indian bowlers if they are struck for boundaries, who spend useless hours on net just doing nothing... But there is something that ensures an immense contentment inside me. I am not mad in love, but I love somebody madly.

It's not that I am never sad or negativities don't shoot me because I am in love... it's not that I don't give a damn to this world because I am in love., it's not that I am affected by the jeers of this world.. But it's just that I have a very special person on this planet, after talking to whom all my pains are vanished, I become abnormally rejuvenated and satisfied. My life has been touched to the core, and there is a big difference in me which only I can realize, or maybe people's around me as well?

'I' am in love, 'I' am in love and 'I' love to be loved...

Throughout these 7 years we both were so much connected to each other we completed 7 years in a relationship. Yes we had millions of break ups but at the end of the day we both needed each other to complete each other. We were now very much matured adult couples. We both were earning as well... Shatabdi joined Hotel Tunga as an front office assistant and I joined my dad's businesses keeping my dream of being a cricketer aside just because I wanted my dad to be happy even thou we both still were the same 'Father & Son' but his designation was changed from being a 'Father' to being 'Boss'...

My father was kind to me whenever we both had a word but still I wasn't able to connect to him, there were many reasons for It., was it because he loves his elder son much? Or is it because of me that I have to quit cricket to support him in his business? Even thou he never said me to quit it... But I always wanted that he should know that I sacrificed my carrier just because he needed me, my brother was working for some other company as a sales manager, he recently quitted from our family business just because of the arrogant and rude behavior of my dad, He was like that and he is like that, even if anything goes wrong because of him he use to blame me:

"You are the reason we don't have any growth in our business"

"I don't know why you are here you should quit my office"

and many such things which use to hurt me like am getting pierced in my heart from someone no one can expect, I never said anyone regarding this neither I opposed him, after all he is my dad am suppose to listen to whatever he says.. It was Shatabdi who can make out anything from my voice if am sad or happy...

Soon it was Shatabdi's birthday.

We have celebrated many of her and mine birthday together and each her birthday was as special as the first one...

25th August

I woke early and after getting dressed, I went to a florist. Like a crazy lover I roamed outside the centre one mall, waiting for it to open doors. Thankfully for me, it opened sharp at 8 am. I was the only shopper in the thousand-yard store!

I gave the florist a bunch of thirteen roses and said "Ah! Pack all these" and I was busy writing a birthday note for Shatabdi...

"Sure" she said

"thank you" I said and ran out as soon as I got the '13 Rose Bouquet'

Things had been changed in past 7 years now I don't have to catch buss or a rickshaw to visit her. As I got my own car a 'Ford Figo' which was also chosen by Shatabdi... Each and everything in it was of her choice. The color of the car - stereo system - the pattern of the seat – the mag wheels – and even the key chain...

It was 8:30 am when I reached outside her place. I called her on the cell phone.

She picked up the phone and said "Hello"

I didn't say anything but began to whistle the Happy Birthday tune.

On the other side I could hear her giggling and then laughing alternately.

"Happy Birthday, Sweetheart!" I finally whispered into the phone

"Thank You, Madz!" she said. She was still laughing. "It's so sweet of you!"

She had plenty of nicknames for me, from my already nick name of Maddy she managed to shorten it further to Madz. But it did not stop there. She would often distort it further at her will- it mostly depended on her mood. The most common nickname she came up with was Shona... And at times I even got to hear Idiot-jerk-stupid-kamina. When she wanted to sound extra cute so that I would take her for a drive she use to say "Babu-u-u-u-u-u" yes with those extra "U's"

"Now will you come out or should I come in?" I asked.

"Oh, are you outside? Here?" she asked excitedly.

"Yes baby!" I said.

Minutes later I saw her running out of her building. She was in her nightdress and her hair was not made, her face wasn't fresh as I had seen earlier. But she looked cuter than she looked before. It's good to see beauty in its purity, untouched.

She was smiling. I knew she had not brushed yet but her teeth were shining white I'd most admired in her and also told her about.

As she came closer to me, I pulled out the bouquet from the back seat of the car and presented her.

"Happy Birthday once again!"

I hugged her and kissed her cheek; she looked at the bouquet for a while and looked back at me, still smiling.

"There is a note in it," I said.

"Arey haan Shona! Ismein toh kuch hai!" she exclaimed, her eyes twinkling with anticipation. She took her sweet time in reading the note, standing a foot away from me to read peacefully. She stood in her favorite posture- legs straight and head tilted over the left shoulder.

I wrote a few lines about her to make her feel good.

When she had finished reading, she rushed to me with open arms and hugged me tightly.

"Thank you so much Shona" she said smiling. We talked for a while after which she went inside again...

And that's when I messaged her "U should now read what's on the back of the note"

In the next minute she replied: "oh! Toh ye baat hai, love you babu-u-u-u! Give me half an hour"

The back of the note was written: ***"We are going 'Matheran' right now get ready and come fast am waiting. I know you don't have office today and tomorrow. Don't ask me how I managed to know that."***

This wasn't the first time we were going there but was the first time as it was an overnight picnic, and we were going because it was our favorite destination to visit.

And then she came it was 9:40 in the clock her half an hour extended to "ONE and a half an hour" I didn't said anything to her it was her birthday she could have taken more 5 hours if she wanted, 'I don't know why girls take so much time to get ready?'

While we reached Matheran at 11:10 am. As we have been there many times in our past 7 years, so it was just like visiting our farm house so I booked our hotels and all other stuff previously thru phone.

Matheran is the smallest hill station in India Matheran's proximity to many metropolitan cities makes it a popular weekend gate away for urban residents., Matheran, which means 'forest in the forehead' of the mountains is also an eco-sensitive region it is Asia's only automobile- free hill station..

After reaching at our hotel we got freshen up and went to the near market as Shatabdi wanted to shop something for her, we decided we'll have a look at some points over here and then after having dinner we'll go back to the hotel rooms.

And we did the same we visited some of the points such as Alexander point- monkey point- panorama point which provided as a 360 degree view of the surrounding area. Then we visited the charlotte lake, and then her favorite Celia point where there is water fall... we both rested near a bench which gives a great look of the water fall we were so lost in the view and talking to each other that we forget what the time is..

"Dost, 8 baj gaye chalna hai yaw main jau" the guy whose horses we were riding said to me standing from my backside...

"haan haan chal we are coming give us 5 minutes" I said as I was awaken from his voice form our lost world, "let's go baby aren't you hungry" I said I patted her stomach,

"Am damn hungry but I want to have you my cutie-pie" she said with a curve in her smile and her naughty eyes said everything.

"Surely you can have me baby but first let me have something, bakra halal karne se pehle use kuch khilate hai" I replied as I knew what her intentions was and we both laughed.

We had our dinner as she ordered most of the sea food... being a Bengali says it all...

We were back at our room.

We both changed into our night dresses. I switched on the television to see is there any nice cricket match to view...

She went through the DVD collection of the hotel disappointed that she could only find mindless action movies, just the kind she hated., disappointed, she asked me to pick one, I was not in the mood to watch movies neither she was I knew she is trying to tease me.,

I was still trapped her words, words she didn't realize could affect me the way they did. She was always good with words.

"Do you mind?" she said, as she slipped right next to me. Holding me tight and trying to close her eyes...

"Are you sleepy" I said as I still remembered her words *'I want to have you my cutie-pie'*

"No am not, but you are so busy watching television that you forget there's a hot birthday girl with you in the room as well" she said angrily

"No baby it's not like that" I said switching off the television set and throwing the remote away from us.

"Leave me don't touch me" she said and held me even tighter.

"So what am I suppose to do, Bhangda?" I said confused, she smiled and kissed my chest and said "light band karo ab jao" pointing me towards the switch board,

As I dimmed the lights and came back to her I was about to say something...

She silenced me with a kiss. Her lips felt like warm honey. She kissed, for a long time, holding my face in her hand, our tongues gently touched. I placed my left hand on her cheek.

She guided my right hand to her back. Her dress was backless, and I felt smooth skin.

She removed my grey T-Shirt. I tried to remove her dress but it was too complex a garment for me to understand. I tugged at it, and then gave up. She unzipped a side zipper and stepped out of it.

We embraced. We kiss. We touched. We caressed. We reached the bedroom, the bed. Our lips never stopped kissing. Our hands never stopped touching.

Every moment felt special as we made love, our eyes met. Both of us felt strong and vulnerable at the same time. I saw tears in her eyes.

"You okay baby?" I said

She nodded. She brought her face close to my ear to whisper

"More than okay. I'm great" she said. "And you?"

"More than great" I said.

We cuddled afterwards. She slept. I didn't. I looked at her all night.

I realized this is only when daylight seeped in through the windows.

I turned towards her. Her skin glowed in the morning light. Her eyes were shut.

"You sleeping?" I asked her.

She nodded hugged me and kept sleeping.

I wished last night didn't have a morning.

NEXT DAY MORNING

We left from Matheran

We hardly talked about the view of Matheran on the way back. She was too busy poking fun at how spoilt I was, and how mature she is. *'Obviously in the couch'*

"Here," she said, as we stopped outside decrepit flat seemed like they would fall apart any moment, the buildings were stained form water that seeped through their walls, the paint was wearing off and the walls were scaly, they were a wreck.

"Accha which one is your flat I only know the building of yours" I said

"Ohh, right there," she pointed to a balcony with clothes hanging on a clothesline, with a smile on her face.

As I saw her smile, I could not remember the last time I had smiled looking at my house after a long day. She was smiling and I was alone, she understood what's in my mind and said "Baby I love u naa I'll be your *mother* hamesha chalo acche bacche ki tarah hug do mujhe" she said hugged me sideways as we were sitting in the car..

"Thank you sweetheart" I said and I cried even she began to cry and wipe my tears form my cheeks and kissed me again and again to show her love to show me that am not alone.

She knew me very well she knew I always miss my mom each and every moment of my life...

"I MISS MY MOM" I said and busted into tears again she held me very tight as if she'll never let me go..

When my mom passed away I was too young., she lost her battle against cancer, I didn't know I have lost my mother till certain age, I tried to prepare myself for the loss, but nothing prepares you for death, nothing prepares you for absence, *with her death a small part of me died too.* I don't use to cry, I lived in denial, I thought I would wake up someday and find her sitting beside my bed.

It had become impossible for me to survive without her, the silence used to drive me crazy, I used to shout at nights and talk to her pictures in hanging on one of the wall at my home only to realize that she was no longer there.

I used to remember all those times when my mother had a word with me after coming back from the hospital, I couldn't recollect any of those, I was such an unlucky guy I don't even remember what she use to call me.. I used to regret every such moment when I was unable to do so., the uncelebrated Mother's Day, and her Birthday's were the days when I use to go at the terrace of my building and cry my heart out and wish her seeing up in the sky. 'I STILL DO', however, in that

Incomplete house, and in my empty life, I could have done anything to have her rest my head on her shoulder and put me to sleep. I loved my mom and I missed her every day. She left a huge void on my life. She was everything to me, **'My Only Family'**

"Mom I Miss You I Really DO"

I wish heaven had a phone so I could hear her voice one last time…

ACT SIX

Date With The Devil 1ˢᵗ Innings

It was a Sunday afternoon; I was at the DY.Patil Sports Stadium playing cricket with my friends... Even thou I left cricket in a professional way but I loved the game it was something I could never say no... from the past 7 years I lost many of my old friends and with few I was in touch but just like an acquaintance.. Over the years I built up new friends they were. Wasim, Aabid, Vijay, Neeyaz, Prafful & Rocky., Rocky was my cousin but we were friends first we both got along together very well from the day he shifted from Lucknow to Mumbai for his studies,

Shatabdi and I rarely use to meet on Sunday's, even she changed in last seven years her family became an believer to Christianity religion, I never asked her why is that so.. I never ever said anything to her about it because it was not her religion which I loved it was 'HER', every Sunday she uses to visit church with her family for bible study, even she got few new friends over the years Radhika, Nitesh, Mehul, Nilesh, Anjum, Aakash and many more form her college... Sunday was the only time for me to go on a date with my second love and that was **"CRICKET"**

Every Sundays we use to play cricket whole day from morning 9:00 am till we were able to see the ball... it was same day as always we were batting first me and Wasim were suppose to be the openers of our team Wasim was an extra ordinary player he was someone I wanted to be as a batsmen..

That day we were batting very well even I was in very good touch Wasim scored an 58 of 26 balls before he got out, I was still on the field not out on 38 of 23 balls with Vijay on the non strike.

"Maddy your phone is vibrating" Neeyaz shouted from the boundary line

"Who's call its is?" I shouted back as he was standing almost 80 meters away from me

"It's Shatabdi's" he said and went back to his seat as he was the next batsmen to be in

She didn't go for bible study? I thought in my mind

Again Neeyaz shouted with even louder voice "I called her back she said tell him to call me as soon as he gets free"

"Ok ok" I said with a thumbs up.

She never calls me before 4pm on Sundays and it's still 11:30 I was confused with that one single call... "Bro you need to concentrate" Vijay said to me as I was looking lost.

Soon I scored a half century in the next five balls I faced... As I waved my bat towards my team mate Neeyaz was standing with my cell phone in his hand and trying to show me something...

"Now what?" I said in sign language enough to Neeyaz understand what I mean

"She's calling again and again" he shouted...

Soon I realized there something wrong otherwise she wouldn't call me this much...

I decided to go off field... so I declared myself Retired Hurt...

The score board shows Maddy: 52 of 28 balls Retired hurt*

As I came back I got my cell phone back from Neeyaz its showed 9 miss calls and I called Shatabdi instantly... The first call went unanswered and so do the second one now I was even more worried... I called her again... it was the third time the ring went on for almost 25 seconds and then she picked up the call...

"Love you" she said very sweetly... as soon as I heard her voice I was sure there's nothing wrong...

"What Happen? Why don't you pick up the call as soon as I call you?" I asked as I was irritated calling her again and again...

"Arey baba I was applying nail polish naa" she said

... I mean what's wrong with girls first they call you an number of times as if they are in big trouble and when you try to call them back they are busy In applying nail polish...

"What the fuck?, so I am an idiot calling you in between of my match retiring myself just to make sure everything's ok with you, even thou my team needed me badly at crease" I said at a one go..

I was angry because I could have made a century 'coz I was playing quite well.

"Even I need you, I was missing you" she said very innocently like a kid who wants a toy from a toyshop,

I calmed down myself and said "You didn't went for bible study?"

"You started shouting before I could say anything" she said.

"Ok baba I am sorry, chalo now tell me why didn't you go, any problem?" I said as sweetly as I could have said

"Naa aaj mood nai tha, I said mom am going to take rest" she said in happy voice.

"Okay, I thought there's something wrong I left my inning in between that's why so you should take rest baby" I said as I wanted to resume my innings again.

"No, I want you to meet me now" she said ordering me.

"Now, but where sweetheart? It's really hot today" I said I was making excuses because I didn't wanted to miss my cricket.

"Why don't you say directly that you want to play cricket and you don't want to meet me" there she was right on target she said it in a loud voice her anger was visible thru her voice itself.

I was caught red-handed so I tried to make some excuses in which I failed miserably, and as she wanted at last I said "Okay Baba, get ready am coming to pick you up"

"Better, Love You My Cricketer" she said and disconnected the call.

"I need to go sorry brother" I said Wasim as I was moving towards the main gate of the stadium. "Asshole! I knew it you bastard" he said as now they have to play one player short form their team.

"Best luck, and do bowl well you moron" I said and walked out.

"Am standing outside your building come fast" I said to Shatabdi on the phone.

"Wait naa give me 20minutes" she said

"What is this first you call me and tell me to come as soon as possible and now 20 more minutes! What's wrong? Is the devil not letting you come out sooner" I said as I was sure am not going to wait more twenty minutes in such a hot day.

"Accha do one thing you come in" she said

"What?" at first I was not sure what I heard she was calling me inside her home...

"yaw baby, come in" she said again.

"But..." I was saying as she interrupted in between and said "don't worry nobody's at home"

As soon as I heard '*nobody's at home'* I was excited as if I have scored a century sitting back in my car away from the stadium...

"Coming" I replied and rushed to at her place...

This was first time I was at her place... her house was on the ground floor... as I entered her home I saw fish tank on the left hand side with two gold fish in Shatabdi always said me about it... although it was my first time but I felt I have been here like 'Déjà Vu', but actually it was because Shatabdi described her house so well each and everything so perfectly, I sat on the sofa in her living room she gave a glass of water from the kitchen just behind the sofa and went inside to change, the bedroom was on the right hand side form the sofa.

I sat there for few minutes and then I stood up and went inside, the bedroom was locked form inside, I knocked the bedroom Dorr and said "anybody here?"

"No no ones at home shut your mouth up and be seated let me get ready" she said from inside.

"I can help you" I said and laughed a bit...

"Accha beta?" she said from inside and suddenly the door of the bedroom was unlocked and she came out.

"Ohh oh looking fabulous" I said as I couldn't manage to look off she was wearing a white dress with red prints on it, she looked so beautiful in Indian wear, just like the perfect girl...

We came in the living room I sat on the sofa she went inside the kitchen and came outside with a water bottle and handed it to me., I took it and tapped on the sofa next to me make her sit beside me.. She was looking beautiful so I couldn't resist and...

I kept the bottle of the water on the table next to the sofa and instinctively leaned into her I put my hand across her shoulders and she didn't brush it off, a little later, she slid down and connected her lips with mine, I firmly held her in my arms and turned her over so that I could be on top of her, she allowed me to. Then I gently took her lower lip within mine and watched her closing her eyes. I kissed her passionately.

'We kissed each other..."

We were so much lost in our self... that we didn't heard the door bell rang for the first time and then it rang again and again... we both stood up from the sofa.. And were looking each other quietly and numb for sometime... I was still holding her hand... and then she said "I am dead" with tears in her eyes... I won't lie even I was dam scared at that time but I managed to look calm at said ...

"Don't worry you just go inside the bedroom and lock it from inside as if you are still changing"

"Are you sure this is going to work?"She said as the door bell rang once again.

"Do you have any other plan?" as I said she ran inside the bedroom and locked it from inside...

I moved towards the main door and opened it... it was her younger brother Nabendu I was still worried that he has caught me red handed with her sister but still I was happy it's not her mother the devil of my dreams,

"What are you doing at my home" Nabendu said in a confused voice he knew me as we were in the same school and college as well, and also he knew about 'OUS'

"Nothing I said came to pick up Shatabdi she is changing inside form the last half an hour" I said '*half an hour*' just to let him know that we both were in different rooms...

"Why it took so much time to you to open the door?" he said as he was confused if from half an hour we both are in different room what I was doing when he ranged the door bell for almost 6-7 times

'Making plans to get rid of you bastard' I thought in my mind...

"The lock is very confusing I was unable to open it, you see am not a family member of this house naa that's why" I said giving another excuse to him...

"So don't even try to be," he said and continued "where is di?" I pointed towards the bedroom he charged towards the bedroom knocked the door and said "tini ekhane ki karache" (what is he doing here)

Nabendu thought I don't understand their language but I was very good at Bengali thanks to Shatabdi it was my like my second language. I couldn't speak Bengali but understand it very well…

"Tini amake nite esechilena" (he came to pick me up) she said from inside.

"Tai take baire damrano" (so make him stand outside) he said again leaning towards the door.

Suddenly she opened the door and came and said "He is my friend I can't make him stand outside in sun to wait for me, do I say anything when your friends visit here?" she was angry at him, and I was happy she was taking my side..

"Apani cana na" (do whatever you want) he said and came in the living room I was expecting some harsh words from him but he didn't he came wore his pair of shoes slammed the door as hard as he could and went out.

'I wonder why he came.'

"Now what" I said as I was bit relief

"Be prepared" she said with one hand on his forehead…

"Prepared? For what?" I asked her as I was confused…

"He'll tell this to mom for sure" she said and I understood what she meant...

"Don't worry everything's going to be ok" I said and kissed her forehead she hugged me and from that hug I could have make out how scared she was...

Same day at 6:00 pm I was at my home… I got a call from Shatabdi's number I received the call…

"Hello is this Mukesh?" a lady said voice similar to Shatabdi

"Yes! Who's this?" I said as somewhat I got an idea who she was...

"This is Shatabdi's mother this side, could you please come to our place right now?" she said or she ordered I was confused as I was talking to the devil of my love story... Shatabdi always said she hated me when ever Shatabdi talked a bit about me...

"Yes off course aunty, I'll be there in half an hour" I said and from now on, I'll refer to her as aunty, as now it's become a homely matter for me.

After the call and before going to meet the lady of my nightmares along with the lady of my dreams, I was nervous. "This is going to be a major interview, I couldn't even imagine failing in it" I thought in my mind.

I dressed myself as well as I could, didn't use musk to prevent the streak of sneezes from my beloved, and shaved my cheek of every strand of hair to look elegant. I was sure I was going to talk about my marriage, without the knowledge of my family members.

When I was ready to leave my place I was in the car, I got a call from Shatabdi's number again...

I picked up said "am on my way aunty give me 10 minutes" as I was worried to be late...

"It's me you idiot" Shatabdi said and I was relieved... And I shot her many questions regarding the meeting...

"Did Nabendu said everything?"

"Why she called me?"

"From where she got my number?"

"What am I suppose to talk?" I was so nervous I even asked

"If your mother started to hit me am I suppose to fight back or surrender?"

We had a talk for five minutes and she hanged up...

I was given four very direct advices, failing which I could have landed myself in trouble.

1. Don't talk about cricket.
2. Don't disclose your real earnings.
3. Don't crack jokes. You suck at it.
4. When in house, don't try to take my help. Being an independent all her life, she likes men who are independent and brave, unlike you.

I was hopeful to easily follow the first two guidelines, but I'd never had the practice of the third one and the considering the quality of my jokes, I feared that I would be mercilessly butchered, if not by the irate mother, then her daughter. And about the fourth one, I was not sure what she said so I just 'let it go' in cricket we say 'Well Left'.

I reached their place, and pressed the call bell... the same bell which crated this much of scene. Aunty opened the door with her typical cold face staring hard at mine. At first, I got so frightened, that I mumbled an indistinct sorry for pressing the call bell. She replied, "What?" thereafter, I gathered control over myself and said "Namaste" with folded hands. It was only after I said Namaste that I was asked to come inside.

I got seated on the sofa and began staring around as if am on some other planet...

Aunty seated in front of me accompanied by her friend 'Kanchan aunty'

"So Mukesh how are you?" she said her cold face exhibited some warmth but just for few seconds.

Just then Shatabdi arrived from her room. Her wet hair and freshness told me that she just come from her bath.

"So Mr. Pandey, what were you doing here in the afternoon?" aunty shot her first arrow.

Mr. Pandey! Was it a compliment for my sleek attire or was it subtle mockery?

"Aunty…" I fumbled with words. It was as though my tongue was walking on a steep road of a Mario-like video game wait a lot of words in the air that it had to jump and acquire, but instead it toppled and rolled the slope, without encountering any words.

"Aunty…" I coughed, looking at Shatabdi, who hinted me to go ahead and break the awkward pause.

"Aunty" it was the third time I was saying that word and I felt like pulling my tongue out and hanging me with it tied to the ceiling fan. Aunty was now irritated, her head clearly showed wrinkles and she was about to speak something when I nervously sped through my monologue:

"I want to marry your daughter. I mean not now, but in a while, and I want you to stop searching a daughter for her, ummm… I mean a groom for her. I'm perfect for her. She also likes me. You also know that, don't you?"

She didn't reciprocate and with her sharp look, I could understand that I'd erred of woofing like a dog in a lion's den. I was waiting for the lion to roar.

"That's not the answer of my question, and for your kind information am not searching any groom for her am not in a hurry to get her married, and one more thing she doesn't likes you get that" she said in sharp voice and as I expected the lions roar...

But I only thing which came in my mind was her last words 'She doesn't likes you'

"What?" I said I was confused. Seeing me confused Shatabdi interrupted in between and said to her mom

"I like him mom, I love him I want to get married to him"

"Apani bhitare yana" (you go inside) her mom said shouting at her and she went inside...

"So tell me what you were doing here in afternoon?" she repeated her question again...

"I was doing nothing I came to pick her up, but it was hot outside so I decided to wait inside your living room just where I am sitting right now, what's wrong in that?" I said it so confidently that she believed I was doing nothing at the time her son ranged the door bell.

"Okay, leave that, so you want to marry my daughter and you think am going to let you do that?" she said and hit her next arrow.

"Yes I want to, what's wrong in that also? We both love each other, and most of all am going to keep her happy always as she is now with me, don't you want your daughter to be happy?" I said...

"See it's not like that you are a Brahmin and we are Bengalis plus we are believers if you know that, I am not giving my girl to someone who isn't a believer or a Bengali" she said in a normal tone trying to make me understand...

"So you are talking about religion? I don't believe in it" I said...

"Ohh, matured boy haan! Okay tell me how much you earn?" she said as soon she said that I thought of the second advice given by Shatabdi (Don't disclose your real earnings) she knew her mom very well that's why I got this piece of advice from her...

"I earn 40 to 50 thousand a month" I said, actually I lied; in synergy with the advice Shatabdi gave me before arriving there. I only mange to earn maximum amount of 20 thousand per month so nearly I doubled my figures.

"Oh may I ask what you do to earn this much amount?" she asked as I thought she would be impressed by the amount and won't bother asking me from where...

"Am self employed, we have a business of steel building materials we export it all over India mostly in Mumbai and Maharashtra" I said and described her little bit of our family business.

"We? You have a partner in your business?" she asked

"No not a partner actually it's our family business" I said proudly as if our business had million of turnover annually... And that's when she got a point.

"So you don't do anything on your own, our you were not able to do anything on your own so you choose your family business? Am I right Mr.Pandey?" this time it was surely a *subtle mockery.*

"I wanted to help my dad, that's why I choose our family business, and am capable to do many things on my own" I said as I was bit frustrated by her question...

I mean what she thinks of herself... I can't do anything of my own... I was a professional cricketer I earned 10 to 15 thousand per match... I could have said her there itself but I remembered one more advice given by my lady love (Don't talk about cricket) so kept quiet.

"What if your dad doesn't agree with you for your marriage with my daughter" she said and she had point this time because I knew my dad will never ever give permission to do a love marriage.

So that was a Yorker deliver for me… I only managed to say "he'll surely allow I'll talk to him"

And then she came to the point no matter what I said, no matter what I did, no matter how I look, her decision was going to be the same.. And then she said

"Look Mr. Whoever you are" so from Mr. Pandey I was directly exclaimed as Mr. Whoever you are…

And she continued again in her sharp voice…

"I don't care what you and how much you earn, I even don't care what your religion is... But let me tell you one thing there's no chance that you can get married to my daughter" I interrupted her in between…

"But aunty what's the problem we both love each other and we are mature enough to take our own decisions" and then she interpreted me…

"No means No... You can't get married to my daughter go found another girl for you" she said in a loud voice loud enough that even Shatabdi in bedroom could have heard it, and yes she did and I saw her standing near her bedroom tears falling from her eyes I wanted to catch those tears grab her in my arms kiss her forehead and say 'don't worry I'll take you out of here soon'.

"Its okay aunty, I understand you don't like me, but we'll get married soon" I said as a challenge to her… and in response I heard the most brutal words of the day... she said...

"I'll kill both of you if that happens" that's showed me how much she hated me... and then she continued

"You may leave now to never come back"...

I didn't said anything after that I stood up and said "Namaste" again the both the aunty Shatabdi's mother and the other one the mute spectator Kanchan aunty...

As I got out of the door her mother came to close the door I heard Shatabdi's voice form my backside... she said to her mother

"antata take eka glasa jala dite" (At least give him a glass of water) and then her mother said

"Maddy if you want you can have dinner here" as if I am homeless guy and she is offering me dinner... I refused and said...

"Thanks aunty I had enough" folding my hand again in front of her...

And I left form there....

'Soon To Come Back'

After my Date with the Devil got over we didn't met for almost two weeks but the devil couldn't stop my girl as she has to report to her office soon...

And then form that day I never dared to visit her place... no matter how much time she takes to get ready... We were sure about one thing that our parents are not going to support us for the marriage we have to do something ... I remembered the first thing she said after we met...

"Your mother, she is a devil, she'll never let me marry to you" I said...

"Don't say anything about her she is just over protective" she said as nothing was wrong

"So what do you want me to do?" I asked her as we reached to gate of hotel Tunga I came to drop her...

"Take me with you wherever you want, am ready to runaway with you my superman" she said and gave me kiss on my cheek.

I smiled and kissed her as well, and she continued "Haan main toh bhool hi gayi I have mailed my resume to some airlines and even got some good response regarding it, I should do it naa?"

"Do what?" I asked

"I want to be an airhostess" she said… "Off course do it baby you have done your course in aviation academy go for it do let me know when is your interview?" I said as I knew she always wanted to work for an airline and always supported her to do whatever she wanted.

We used to meet at vashi sector-15 near bus stop and use to drop her at her "Indian Aviation Academy" classes in the evening in Nerul. It was memorable time for me when I kept waiting outside at the bus stop while her classes went on for two hours from five to Seven in the evening, it looked stupid but I used to wait for her and that made her smile. And sometimes weird when few people asked me if I needed any help or why I was standing there for so long.

And then after classes we used to go to mini seashore and have some Chinese together.

She was being dependent on me and that I never wanted to make her do. I wanted her independent flying girl who wanted to live with her dreams that she dreamt but never discussed with anyone.

"Interview is in the next month they'll mail me regarding it soon" she said while opening the door of the car...

"Okay sweetheart no issues, now go or you'll be late" I said as she walked out of the car and disappeared in the hotel for her shift.

'After few days she was called for an interview but not in Mumbai but in Kolkata...'

ACT SEVEN

The Bong Connection

Shatabdi was set to go Kolkata for an interview as she was trying to be in the aviation academy. None of us wanted to part ways. And this fact was visible on her innocent face.

That day she visited my home as there was no one there.

"Can I fall sick and stay back here with you?" she asked me, cutely pouting her lips like a kid and as usual letting her head bend sideways.

"No dear" I said and rubbed her cheek with my hands. I didn't want her to suddenly change her focus from her aviation dream to me.

"Common lets go" I said picking her bag up as I was supposed to drop her at the airport

We reached at the Mumbai airport located 1.30hrs far from our place

I parked the car at parking lot and moved along with Shatabdi We moved towards the "Departures Terminal 1B" we were still standing there out; talking when got a call from her friend 'Amrut' asking her to come fast as their flight was in next 1 hours. Shatabdi turned to leave when I pulled out that juice can which I had picked up for her before leaving from my home. Back at my place we had been so busy that we didn't have time for anything else she was overjoyed when I gave the can to her. She felt I cared. I planted a kiss on her forehead and waved a goodbye. She left for her flight. I left for my office.

She was boarding Go-Air flight at 2pm in the afternoon... She messaged me as soon as she reached Kolkata.

She was supposed to stay at her Nani's place as Kolkata being her second home.

We kept exchanging warms SMS's over the phone till late at night, I was very tired, yet I forced my eyes open to read and reply. The anticipation of waiting to receive her next message was tickling me inside. And every time my cell phone vibrated it made my heart pleasantly skip a beat. A bit of anxiety, a bit of fresh romance and a bit of drowsiness had all effectively intoxicated me till sleep overtook my senses.

It was Sunday afternoon. We are watching the same movie on our television, she is at her place and I was at mine. And I am doing this because she sent me an SMS, telling me to watch it.

In the movie, the heroine is packing her bags after having a big fight with her husband.

At this very moment, Shatabdi calls me up. And putting her in that woman's shoes, I don't understand why she said that, "you know what? If someday I am so angry that I want to run away from you, just do a simple thing," I didn't say anything, but she continued . . .

"Simply run to me and give me a tight hug, no matter how much I hit you then, but give me a warm, tight hug. Don't say a word. Just hold me in your arms for some time . . . and a little later, help me in unpacking my bags. Bolo karoge naa?". . . How cutely she use to say "naa" every time she use to say those words I use to fall for her over and over again

We use to chat daily for hours as her interviews were getting postponed due to unknown reason... Her stay of twenty day was now been extended to two months,

We use chat till morning mostly I use to cheer her up because she use to be sad that she is unable to see me and hug me..

Shatabdi: I love you baby, am missing you!

Maddy: ok

Shatabdi: You are so boring and irritating!

Maddy: So are you going to leave me?

Shatabdi: YES!

Maddy: Thank you Bye

Shatabdi: Once again, I was totally nuts to have said a yes to you. Idiot!

And the chats goes on daily someday it was me who use to piss her off or someday she use to do so...

Shatabdi: Promise me you'll always be there for me, to hold me whenever I fall.

Maddy: I promise that if someday you fall, I will help you to get up.

Shatabdi: Thank you so much. I love you.

Maddy: But... I'm also going to laugh. *Hahaha*

Shatabdi: I hate you! Kamine...

And then she ...

Shatabdi: it's so cold here in Kolkata

Maddy: huh! Even here but I bath daily even in this chilling winter

Shatabdi: so sad!

Maddy: Why sad, it's something I am proud of

Shatabdi: Even then your dirty mind couldn't get cleaned! *Hahaha*

Our chats and calls use to go on and on and on... we didn't needed any topic we could have talked on how to talk on phone while talking on phone itself, Ya I know it was stupid but we were in love and its legal to be bit stupid in love.. Actually love demands some stupid things you need to make her smile make laugh and make her feel special at the same time and I was very good at it...

We talked hours and hours a day and missed each other more and more day by day,

"Joker you are, Idiot" she said as I cracked some PJ on the call I was at my office I didn't had any work... She was also at her place as her interview was yet again postponed due to *'don't know why'* reasons

"Why don't you just settle down there itself" I said angrily I was frustrated because her interview has taken almost 2 months now.

"Why you saying this?" she asked me politely,

"So what should I do? Do you even realize it's been two months we haven't seen each other?" I said again in the same tone

"So is it my mistake what can I do this bastard's aren't ready to take the interview, they say 'our HR is out of station and will be interviewing you once he comes back'" she said or almost cried

I knew I said wrong but what other could I have done I was missing her badly I wanted to hug her, as I was only her to share everything I wasn't close to my family not at all. In office also I didn't talked to my dad or if I did it would be only of office purposes.

"What happen Shona you seem to be upset" she said again as I didn't responded to her answer

"Nothing! Am missing you, please come fast" I said and I was in tears.

"Did dad say anything again?" she said and she knew exact reasons every time I get upset.

Most of the time I got to hear from my dad for no reasons, he always thought that I am of no use I never argued with him regarding that as always... Shatabdi said me many times to make my relation stronger with my dad as he is your father and he loves you no matter what happens... But I wasn't ready for it... I was just fulfilling my responsibility of being a son... even thou I was a bad one...

"Okay now don't cry I'll come tomorrow itself, I don't want any job I want you my superman" she said and gave a kiss thru the phone.

"No no no, shut up! You have been there for your interview for almost two months, you have invested so much time now finish your interview get selected and then only step back in Mumbai" I said and laughed.

"I know, but you know what?" she said and continued again "I want to hug you" I could recognize from her voice itself she was missing me a lot and then I decide to visit Kolkata the same day itself.

"Okay my coming today itself" I said as soon as I realized she is missing me badly.

"What?" she asked shockingly and there was a bit excitement in her voice "but how you'll mange where you'll stay, let it be" she said but I knew she'll be more than happy to see me.

"I'll call you in some time" I said and disconnected the call.

I left office and came back home.

"Where are you going?" my elder sister Seema questioned me and I didn't bother replying her I continued to keep my jeans and two t-shirts into the bag.

"Would you tell me or should I call dad?" she threatened me she always use to do that and I use to it.

"Do whatever you want" I said tying my shoe laces.

"What's wrong with you? "She said...

"Am just tiered of your entire question, would you let me leave in piece?" I said.

"Do whatever you want I don't care am going to call dad right away" she tried to threaten me again but I was sure about what I was doing...

"Same to you, and don't make my food, I'll return tomorrow evening" I said and left.

As soon as I left my building I cell phone ranged and I knew whose call it was even before looking at the screen of the cell phone.

I took out the phone in my hand it shows 'Pandey ji' calling... Yes it was dads call obviously Seema called him when she didn't got any answer from me and I was ready for this.

I gathered some courage to receive his call "Hello" I said...

"What the fuck do you think of yourself, how dare you talk to Seema like that, don't know you are just a piece of shit, go back home and say sorry to her" he said as aggressively as he could but it was normal for me I knew his behavior towards me.

"But I didn't said anything wrong I just said don't cook food for me as I am going out today" I said in my defense.

"So you think she's a cook, and you are living in a hotel you can come and go whenever you want" he said rudely.

"When did I say that?" I was confused... but he continued...

"I don't care what you said and what you don't just say sorry to her and go back home you are not going anywhere you rascal" yes this were his words.

"Am sorry but am going out I'll be coming tomorrow" I said and was waiting for another outburst from his side

"Go where you want, you bastard don't ever come back in my house again" he said and disconnected the call...

I was still holding the phone in my hand this was the reason I missed my mom every day, every single moment in my life, This is the reason I say my mom was my only family, this Is the reasons am not close to anyone in my family this was the reason I wanted to end up my life... but Shatabdi was the reason I lived for.. She was everything for me everything... She cared for me like a mother does; she scolded me like a father does... That was the reason we both couldn't live without each other '*I specially*'

I reached airport and paid the taxi and went inside the departure gate.

"Next flight to Kolkata" I said to the girl sitting at the counter of Indigo airlines

"Round trip sir?" she said with a smile on her face.

"Yes, tomorrow evening" I said

She did something in her computer for next 10 minutes and said "Cash or card sir" again with the same smile as if she'll kiss me if there would not been ay glasses between us.

'You are committed you idiot stop thinking bullshit about another girls' I said to myself

"Card" I said and then she continued with the procedure "Sir your flight will be in an hour, may I know when are you planning to come back?" she said. "Tomorrow" I replied again "I know sir can I know at what time?"

"Do you have any flight after 6 from there?" I questioned her and she smiled and nodded "let me check" and then she said "tomorrow at 6:45 is it ok sir?"

"Yup that would be great" I said and handed my ID proof and the debit card towards her.

I got my tickets I moved towards the security check point and then towards the indigo airline counter inside the main gate for the boarding pass.

The next moment I was sitting at the gate A13 to board my flight and then I called Shatabdi again.

"Where have you been till now" she said as I disconnected the call previously and said her that I'll call her back.

"I was busy travelling" I said and smiled.

"Travelling?? No no don't tell me you are coming here?" she said most probably with a smile.

"Am at the airport the flight is at 3:15 I'll land in the city of BONG's in three hours" I said excitedly.

"Oh my god!! You are such an idiot, I love you, I love you, I love you" she was very happy and excited much more than I was.

And she continued "Am going to pick you up at airport see you there".

"Arey talk to me am not in the flight I have 10 minutes still" I said

"Nopes sorry I need to get ready for my prince tada... And thank you so much see you in 3 hours" she said and disconnected the call...

In next 15 minute I was in the flight... and I fell asleep don't know when as soon as the flight took off.

I woke up with the announcement inside the flight.

"Welcome to Netaji Subhas Chandra Bose International Airport"

As they continued with the announcement I took my cell phone switched on it and messaged Shatabdi.

"Just Landed, where are you?"

In the next few seconds I got a message from her:

"Don't worry superman u won't be lost in Kolkata am waiting outside come fast love you"

I replied: **"Give me 10 minutes"**

I came out of the airport in next 15 minutes, as I came out I saw many of the cab drivers standing near the gate holding up the sign board mostly with Bengali surname "Mr.Bose, Mr.Chatterjee, Mr.Chakrobarty" and many such tongue twisters. And I was looking for my Biswas... and future Mrs.Pandey...

And there she was!

My angel, my beautiful one.

Her smile which tried to override my senses. That cute hesitation in her, and in me. Her long untied hair that fell upon her eyes with a gust of wind. Her hand moving across her face, and moving her hair behind her left ear. And the glittering silver earrings she was wearing. Her beautiful face, which mesmerized me. And in that white, off-shoulder top and jeans, her body appeared so perfect, so young, so poised. She was beautiful. I wasn't able to take my eyes off her. Rather, I wanted to stare at her from top to bottom, very slowly- which I actually did...

"This is her," I told myself. "She is mine."

That was a wonderful moment which I have re-lived again and again, as we were seeing each other after almost two months.

She came towards me and hugged me tightly I can never forget that hug and I hugged her back we both kept holding each other for very long until we realize it's not a dream.

"I love you thank you so much for this" she said with her eyes full of tears.

"Hey stupid why are you crying? Zyaada zor se hug kar liya kya maine?" I said and laughed.

"Shut up! Chalo lets go I have decided where you'll stay, and we'll have dinner together"

She said holding my hands and moving towards the taxi stand; unlike Mumbai taxis in Kolkata are painted in full yellow... I didn't say anything and followed her like an obedient child.

"Park Street?" she said to the taxi driver.

"hyam hyam" (Yes Yes) he said.

We sat inside it and moved towards Park Street.

"Park street" what kind of name is that? Am I needed to stay in park or some street?" I asked

"No baby its nice hotel to stay" she said and holed my right hands with her both hands and resting her head on my shoulder.

"Seems like someone was missing me" I said kissing on her forehead.

"Yes this taxi driver was dying to spend a night with you" she said and laughed the taxi driver didn't understood what she said but only saw thru the mirror when he heard 'taxi driver'

"Okay now I got it, you want to spend night with me, you desperate bengalan" I said teasingly her.

"I wish I could I mean who'll miss a chance to get cozy with such a hot guy in this chilling winter" she said moving her hands on my chest.

Suddenly the driver said "Yekhane parka rastaya?" (Where in park street?)

"Parka hotela" (the park hotel) Shatabdi replied.

We reached there in half an hour; I paid the taxi driver and entered the hotel.

It was great hotel to stay I paid at the reception and checked in with an ID proof.

I got a deluxe room the room service boy guided us to the room, We entered the room and the bell boy left by showing me the menu card and other important stuff., So as we decided I ordered dinner for us, as it was Kolkata she said I need to taste the sea food mostly fish. Fish is known as the specialty of Bengali's.

As our order arrived we both had it in the same plate while talking to each other... she talked everything about her nani and her family in Kolkata she wanted me to meet her family specially her naani but I told her if I meet her any of the family members here her mom will get to know about it and then she'll get into trouble,. As we finished our dinner we sat on the corner of the bed she came close to me and held my hands and said

"I missed you so much" before she could say anything I held her hands tightly. All theoretical knowledge doesn't work when love happens. So I preferred just to go with the flow.

She closed her eyes. Her breath took a pace the moment I touched her. All human bodies can't have the same temperature and that's why we feel a special pleasure when two bodies touch. She was quiet and softly pushed her face to me. I touched her lips with my thumb and her lips started quivering. I came closer feel her warmth and gusts of her breaths on my lips. I couldn't control my feelings anymore.

Her warm breaths and her fragrance overruled my senses. I kissed on her forehead and she lifted her head up and allowed me to move to her lips. Before going to her lips, I kissed on her eyes and then cheeks. She held my hand tightly and locked my lips with hers.

I would never express what I felt but the deeper she kissed me, the deeper I fell in love with her. We didn't open our eyes and kissed as long as we could and then we got a pace and continued. I rubbed her lip gloss with my tongue and then she said "I love you"

The moment she spoke, I didn't answer and without taking breath gave her a passionate deep kiss. We both felt like vacuum for a moment, "I love you too; I just want to be with you for the rest of my life"

She opened her eyes, looked at me with full love, "Will you always be with me?"

"You are not alone now, I am with you," I promised her holding her hands tightly in mine.

Few tear drops came from her eyes and those were the drops of happiness.

"What happened" I asked.

"Nothing just..." she smiled...

"Aey Stupid girl come here, I am always with you" she came close and I kissed on those tear drops of her. Her lips were wet now and we had a long kiss that just went on for too long.

"Its 10:00 pm I should leave" she said and stood up to wear her sandals even I didn't forced her to stay because it was too late we headed towards the gate and then towards a taxi.. "Kaali ghat" she said and the driver nodded I ask her should I come to drop her but she declined as there are many relatives of her here in Kolkata somebody will see. She left by saying:

"Tomorrow sharp 12:00 o' clock at the south city mall" I nodded and she left...

Next day we were supposed to meet in the afternoon but I got ready early morning because I had to do so many things to make our last day memorable for us... forever. There are few things which are essential for any departure as I was not sure to stay to meet her family because I was invited with no prior plans. So I bought a chocolate cake, candles and a surprise gift. Gifts are not to show how rich you are, those are to make you remember the moments you spent with that person and we already had a series of memories. I boarded a taxi from Park Street and reached

South City Mall. When I entered the mall, I saw someone entering the Archie's gallery who looked just like her form the back as she hadn't reached so I ignored and considered that it happens when you are in love.

"Where are you?" I asked her over a call.

"Just reaching" she responded. Taking the escalators I reached on the top floor in the food court area. I put the cake and gifts on the table. I was excited but somewhere I was unhappy with departure. Someone came from the back and said- Hello. Yes, I was tracked and caught. The one I saw entering Archie's was Shatabdi instead.

"You are already here" I looked at her.

"I saw you, when you entered the mall, I caught you and I would at every moment Mr.Pandey" being so happy and lively she said.

"I am always ready to be hijacked, Miss. Gorgeous" we laughed.

Love is like a healthy competition, if someone loves you, you try to love more and in counter that person proves you wrong. That makes it lively, cheerful and long lasting. Now you can't just sit at home with lighted candles waiting for your partner. You need to go out, do some hard work and be as active as you're in bed. No one needs to follow other to make their love story best, just make you own.

"But this is not fair. Now go and come after 5 minutes, I did hard work to make it possible, so I won't let it go like this"

"Ok ok, I will go, you crazy creature" she said and left.

She went and I put a candle in centre of the cake, managed everything properly as per the plan and then called her.

"So sweet of you" she looked at me and I could remember all the memories. Sometimes happiness is to do something for someone you love.

"I don't know what's the occasion but you can consider this my farewell" I put my head down in Chinese tradition to welcome.

She became emotional and her eyes were full with tears of love, and I was not going to wipe her tears because these tears were of love, life family, friendship, memories and all the stupid things we did.

"Now cut it" I said as the candle dropped a few drops of wax around. We cut the cake, laughed, and lived few last moments before my departure. Celebrations was not over, she took out a box from her bag and gifted me.

"What's that?" I asked

"Open it" she said with a wink.

"Okay" I smiled

"Hey slowly" she said sitting on the chair.

"I can't. Wow, nice wristwatch. I actually needed it" I looked at her and grinned. She poured love in her eyes, touched my hands, "Don't go" said she.

"You'll be coming back in 10days baby" I patted and pinched her nose. I took a box from a bag in which I was carrying my clothes to visit Kolkata.

"What's in it?" excitedly she asked.

"You can open it" I just smiled. She opened the box in seconds. Girls are actually as fast unwrapping gifts as boys are in taking off their inner wears.

"Oh my god" she was just shocked, it was a beautiful dress which she selected few days before online and I rejected it. She continued with her expressions, "but that time you said it was not good"

"Because I wanted to get this for you and I'd like it"

"You are actually a mad guy. Can't believe but thank you so much shone, your choice is just awesome, this is my best dress now" she looked happy and I wanted to make her so.

We missed each other inside but we decided not to say goodbye because we both knew anyone cried, the other would not be able to go away.

She left to Nani's place and I left towards airport, Back To Mumbai...

ACT EIGHT

Date With The Devil 2ⁿᵈ Innings

Few days after my departure from Kolkata her interview was placed by the airlines. As soon as she finished her interview she was back in Mumbai.

We decided to meet near her college as she wanted to meet some of her friend's from where she completed her graduation ICL college. I picked her up from the bus stop and we headed towards her college in sector- 9A. We reached there in next 10 minutes she went inside the college to call her friends out. I was standing near the main gate of the college and my phone vibrated.

"Coming in 5 minutes sweetheart" she said and disconnected the call.

She came out of the gate with her few friends they were Radhika, Nitesh, Nilesh, and Mehul we all just deciding where to go Shatabdi's phone rang... "Sshhh... it's a call from my brother" she said placing her index fingers on her lips.

"Hello" she said. After a few seconds of call she looked at me and said "Am dead"

"What happed that idiot said something" I asked her moving my hands towards her to hug her. She hit on my hand and said "Look behind" as I turned around I saw her brother Nabendu standing other side of the road. I knew what he would have said to her, her eyes said it all she looked upset and said -

"Bye, Guys see you soon" waved her hand to everyone and came bit near to me and whispered in my ears "Love you and be ready".

'Oh no not again I can't face that devil again who doesn't even behave like a human being I hate her' I thought in my mind and nodded looking at her.

As she crossed the road and both the siblings went to their home. And as it happened previously I was expecting a call from her mother in few hours. I explained her friends about the situation and then even I left from there.

'I didn't know what's wrong with his brother can't he see her sister happy' I thought in my mind lying on the sofa and watching a repeat telecast of a match of New Zealand Vs Australia.

As the commentator said "It's high in the air fielder coming underneath it….." my cell phone vibrated and it showed *'Shatabdi Calling…'* I knew it would be her mother calling me to visit her place again in next half an hour. I couldn't gather enough courage to receive the call and it got disconnected.

'What are you doing, why you are scared to talk to her mother? You have to do this at some point in your life, call her back and say her to brace herself this time you are going to give her back' my heart said and I dialed her number 9833xxxxxx... calling…..

"Hello" an old female voice came from the phone… I knew who she was "Hello aunty" I said.

"Hello Mukesh" she said in a polite tone and that was something confusing for me.

"Sorry aunty my phone was in silent so couldn't receive it at the first time" I said giving an excuse.

"That's ok," she said and continued "I think you know why am I calling you" she said.

"Yes aunty, I know but I was there just to meet Radhika, she is my friend as well" I gave an excuse again. She interrupted in between and said "that's ok I don't have problem with it" I interrupted as soon as I heard '*I don't have problem with it*' "Then what happen aunty" I said in a delightful tone. And then she shot the bullet and said "I need to talk to your parents" as soon she said she wanted to meet my parents I received an 2400 volts of current thru the phone aunty has shot the bullet in the right place no matter what happen I can't say this to dad he'll kill me, moreover last time I had a talk with my dad was when he called me while I was leaving to Kolkata and told me

"Go where you want, you bastard don't ever come back in my house again" but still he was good enough to let me live in his house so didn't wanted him to throw me out of the house.

"Hello, you there" her mother said I was lost in my thoughts, "Ahh… yes aunty sorry the network isn't good was not able to hear you" an excuse again, love made me a great liar I lied to my family every time I met her and now I was lying to her mother… "So 6 o'clock in the evening be here with your father" her mother said this time very loud and clear.

"But my father is out of town" I said and praised myself for making a great excuse… from the past ten minutes I lied almost everything.

"Then n n…." she said and continued again "Okay no issues come here with your elder brother Durgesh sharp at six okay"

I was trapped in my own words, I has happy that I was not suppose to visit her place with my father otherwise I would have hanged myself right there. But I was confused as well.

My brother and I shared an interesting relationship between us nobody could have said that we both are brothers we rarely talked to each other and if I talked to him now he'll surely think I need her help.

'What's wrong in asking help from your elder brother' I was talking to mind. 'What if he says no? What if he tells everything to my dad? *What if?"* I was lost in what ifs.

And then I decided that I need to talk to him but I needed help… I was waiting for Shatabdi's call again I thought she would call again to give instruction like she gave me previously. But she didn't most probably her devil mother didn't allowed her to touch the phone. The last idea came to my mind was to call my friend Wasim and Neeyaz for help me as rocky wasn't in the town.

I called both of them and explained my situation to them and called them to my place as soon as possible. They were there in next half an hour; luckily my brother was also at home. I didn't have the guts to talk to my brother regarding it. So we decided Wasim and Neeyaz will talk to him and convince him to come with me.

My brother was in the bedroom doing something on the computer, Wasim and Neeyaz went inside I stayed back in the hall watching the highlights of the match again... Australian openers we batting quite well just to ensure a good start for the team and I hoped that the two players I sent in bat could bat well to give me a good start before the main bowler (Shatabdi's mother) comes in to bowl, I was a bit stupid I always compared the situations as if this would happen in crocket what would I do... every time my dad use to scold me for no reason I use to remember even Sachin Tendulkar defends when he is not in good form, it's all about hanging in there and make the most of it.

Gilchrisht and Hayden successfully scored a 50 run partnership in just 7 over's for Australia. And there they come my openers and they gave good news that Durgesh was ready to come with me. And was ready to help me I was happy but the battle was just started.

6 o'clock in the Evening:

"Let's go" I said to my brother.

"Yes" he said wearing his shoes. I was dressed very well and I made sure that my brother also looks well enough

We reached Shatabdi's place on time. You have to be on time just to impress your in-laws that you are a perfect guy, if you don't value time, time won't value you. So here we were standing in front of the door.

A wooden door which had written 'Nikhil. Biswas' '01' written on it. And then I rang the bell...

'Today it's going to be much better' I thought in my mind as I saw Shatabdi opened the door.

"Come in" she said.

Me and my brother entered her house and placed ourselves on the sofa next to the fish tank. Like previous visit the devil was sitting in front of us again till now she didn't spoke a word but I was ready to take her bullshit as she didn't know what love is.

"Hello beta" she said looking at my brother. *'Excuse me am your son-in-law not him'* I wanted to say it as she didn't said me 'Beta'.

"Hi, Aunty how are you" my brother said.

"Am good beta how are you have something" she said and picked up the plate placed on the table.

"No aunty thank you" he said.

"So you might know why I have called you here" she said and continued "Does your brother knows about it?" she said looking at me.

"Yes aunty that's why he is here with me, to talk about me and Shatabdi" I said in confidence as I had my elder brother's support but then...

"Okay! So Durgesh do you also have girlfriend?" her mother asked.

"Yes aunty I had but we broke up" my brother said. And I knew about who he was talking.

"Why did you broke up with her" she got the opportunity to get on the top.

"Because I knew my father will never accept our relation" he said and I was like *'what the fuck Bhai ye abhi hi bolna tha'*

Now she got a point and grabbed the opportunity to kick my ass "See learn something from your brother he sacrificed his relation just because he didn't wanted to hurt his parents, and you?"

"Aunty I understand why he did that his scenario was complete different, I know in my case dad won't have any issue" I had a glass of water kept the glass on the table and said my brother looked at me shocking.

"Accha, you tell me Durgesh will your father accept your brother's relationship and agree for his marriage with my daughter" she questioned my brother.

And then what my brother said was enough to make me look like a looser.

"NO Never, I said him this but he doesn't listens to me" my brother said looking at me and then at Shatabdi mother.

No I knew I have lost the conversation my card has played against me. '*Why did you say that, you could have lied*' I looked completely lost I looked up near the bedroom Shatabdi was standing with her hand on her forehead. And gesturing me '*what have he said*'. I said nothing and sat there quietly for some time my brother and the devil had conversation on many things later on regarding our religion their religion what he does what is our family business and many things I wasn't interested in the so called interview now. Because I knew whatever I say now will be considered as my desperation to get married to her daughter. She got what she wanted and finally she said to me.

"So as I have told you previously you both should stay away from each other, as your family is also against it"

"Aunty I wanted to say something" I said in a very low voice.

"What?" she said.

"Whatever happens no matter who is against us I don't care if it's you or my brother sitting next to me we will get married to each other" I said and this time not in a low voice but very confidently.

I looked at Shatabdi and she silently said *'I love you baby'* I could read her lips.

"Okay will see" she said in anger.

"Thanks for the water this time" I said and stood up.

"Make your brother understand, you are capable of it" she said to my brother.

"Surely aunty I'll talk to him" he said and we walked out of that slaughter house.

'To Never Come Back'

"Daddy kabhi nahi manenge u know that very well" my brother said to me as we walked towards the car.

"I don't care and thank you for pouring kerosene into the fire thanks a lot" I said him in a taunting way and drove back to home.

ACT NINE

Just Us

The days were normal but the nights were too cold, next morning when I was rolling in my cozy bed, my phone rang with arrival of her call, I charged up. Clock said 8:20am. I answered her call. She replied with a cheerful voice, her voice chocolaty that I liked most to make my day, "Good morning Shona!"

"Good morning" I replied, deliberately groggy.

She suddenly said, "Are you sleeping? Get up now, aren't you heading to office?"

"I'll, its only 8:20 am, I have almost one hour" I covered myself in the blanket in the cold morning.

"Almost one hour left and you're still in bed?" she screeched.

"yes" I said proudly, coming more close to microphone as I wanted to hug the moment in my bed, shrank in bed.

"Get up now" she said again.

"Baii. Okay 20 min aur" I said warily and wanted her to order me to get up.

"Beta, get up. It's not good for health to sleep like this, okay" she said. I snorted.

"Argh! Get up means get up" she repeated. It feels special when someone wakes you up early in the morning and you give all the reasons not to wake up.

"Yeah good night bye!" I moved my fingers to cut the call.

"Wait! Okay listen come to the window now" she said as she is the most innocent girl I have ever met. When a girl acts innocently, there must be a reason behind. I was shocked.

"What?" I was awakening now.

"Maddy, I said come in your window" Shatabdi ordered, I walked towards the window. The cold wind rushed towards me, a feeling of cold gentle bliss that a splash of cold water could never give. I breathed deeply.

"Okay. I'm at the window. What now?" I asked feverishly.

"Now Dance" she said and burst out laughing.

"Ah! How can you do this to me?"

Still laughing, "How do you feel now?" the wind poked every cell it could. I was shivering. However, felt something different and why not, this happened first time with me, yes I woke up so early.

"Ya Very Good thank you" I said bit annoyed.

"I was just kidding, babu. Now get ready for office" she said.

I sighed, said "ok", and hung up. I walked and almost jumped with ecstasy, the energy had nothing to do with the fresh air. I rolled in the bed again, hugged pillow and closed my eyes for few seconds, it was pleasant to sleep in last half an hour, always like heaven. Last ten minutes are always most important, either it's before examination or waking up early morning.

We use to talk like Romeo- Juliet or any other lover would do...

"Hey Shatabdi, you are the best girl that I know, I just want something in return" I used to say.

"What do you want from me?" she usually replied.

"I can have your hug which is priceless for me"

"Shut Up, you are a mad guy"

I tried to make her happy, my crazy talks and her stupid replies, we were not aware but somewhere we were making new memories. We were making the golden nest of our LOVE, true, deep, and strong and crazy of course.

"Would you always be with me?" she asked

"No, I can't promise that" I said and burst into laughter.

"Then get lost" she said.

We used to laugh. Good sense of humor is important to know about a person, to handle and to make your different identity form others. Sitting with aunties and sisters actually, I could try and understand girls and their feelings – what they like, how they think and what they feel. She was childish; she was dependent, careless and a lot more. She used to forget to have milk in the morning, never had anything before sleeping and I always shouted and vice versa.

When I cared, I cared like a mother and listened as a father, when she shared her secrets, she shared as a best friend and when she cried, I was always there to pamper her. We were not making any new definition of life, love and dedication; we just lived the way we both wanted to live.

I didn't give her any chance to miss me. It was tough but manageable. We used to talk till late night. Sometimes my dad caught me talking to someone outing my pillow on my head in the bed. That time I had pretend, "Nothing, just listening songs" there is nothing without risk and I was ready to give anything in return to get her presence around me. Not everything but few things are surely fine in love and war.

ACT TEN
The She Factor

Years passed as we fell deeper and deeper in love now, it was the time that every exclaimed us as the *'Best Couples'* they know. Everyone knew about us, we were in love and we were crazy, we did every possible thing that a couple can do. Sometimes Joker, sometimes Singer, sometimes her Hero... EVERYTHING I was. When she used to wake up, I welcomed her with my smile. Whenever she felt alone, I was there to hold her in my arms. Whenever she felt bored, I even danced in front of her, how crazy I was but I was happy to be like that just for her.

Only thing left was to get married and have children we even decided the name of our kids. If it's a boy his name would be "Rudra" and if it's a girl her name would be

"Priyanka" the girls name was my choice as I was a very big fan of Priyanka Chopra the bollywood actress.

One fine day my cell vibrated and showed a notification *"Message on Face book"* I opened it and it was message from an unknown girl named 'Priyanka Verma' I didn't know that she'll become such a big part of my life.

The message said: ***"Hi stranger, was going thru some profile found your profile quite interesting, we both have same hobbies so just sending a Hi!"***

"Same hobbies?" I thought in my mind and click on ***"View Full Profile"***

She was holding a German Sheppard puppy in her hands wearing a green top, pouting her lips towards the puppies as if she going to kiss the dog, her hair tied in pony tail, a fair complexion girl with big beautiful eyes. She was Beautiful.

Then I looked for the hobby she was talking about and clicked on *'About Me'*

"Hahahaha, seriously" I laughed and thought in my mind. Her hobby was 'playing cricket' and singing and blah blah blah…

I knew she was talking about 'Cricket' because I had only one hobby and it was cricket.

I replied: "Hey stranger that's strange you play cricket! So even am sending you a hi!" in just few seconds she replied I guess she was online that time.

Priyanka Verma: "Hey, yes of course I play cricket, why girls can't play this game? >:o"

Me: "of course they can… good to hear that you play cricket."

Priyanka Verma: "so you play which level, I mean have you played state level or nationals or any club"

Me: "No I haven't played state level but yes I have played for few clubs"

Priyanka Verma: "oh that's great then you must be a very good player ;)"

Me: "Ya Kind off"

Priyanka Verma: "Hey I got to go in office will message you later ☹"

Me: "yup! Bye take care"

Priyanka Verma: "and yes I have sent you the friend request do accept it babyeiii ☺"

Priyanka Verma Is Offline.

I accepted the friend request. And it showed. ***"Priyanka Verma and Maddy Pandey"*** are now friends.

It's strange how social media has changed our lives forever, we get to know and talk to new peoples around the globe and sometimes next to our door without even knowing each other, it has its own advantages and disadvantages.

Shatabdi never believed in social media, she had a face book account which she use to keep deleting in twice every month.

I told Shatabdi about Priyanka chats and teased her saying "Now my fan following is growing day by day"

"Accha beta, show me her profile picture" Shatabdi said. "Here" I said opening my face book on my mobile phone and passed my phone to her.

"Oh I know why she messaged you" she said and smiled in a naughty way.

"Why?" I said

"Can't you see she love animals" and she burst into laughter.

"Oh hello she must have seen my profile picture and would have gone crazy over it and messaged me because of that" I said like a self obsessed guy and she was still laughing.

"yaw yaw I know my man is dam hot any girl can go crazy over him" she hugged me and placed a kiss over my right cheek. And said "But she is cute and I know you accepted her friend request just because her name is Priyanka" and she smiled.

"Sort of, I just love this name" I said and we both laughed.

From that day I chatted with Priyanka daily and I always told Shatabdi about it. Priyanka was from Andheri where I use to live when I was a kid.

I remember some of my memories with my mom in that Andheri's house it wasn't easy for me to remember my days with my mom as I was to small when she was there with me, the one memory I remember form that house is 'Once she was scolding me for some issue and she was sitting on the floor she held my hand and pulled me towards her to make me sit beside her, but unfortunately my leg slipped and my forehead landed on the floor and I had a big injury, my mom took me in her arms and ran towards the Dr. crying throughout the medication I had thirteen stitches on left side of my forehead which I remember as a mark to be cherished forever that was something my mom gave me and I'll have it till die'.

It was way back when I was just 5-6 years old but for now we all grew up, and it felt like it happened yesterday. It was my sister Seema's wedding and I was off to my native place for it.

18/04/2012.

The date when my sister got married, when she got married I was the one who was most relief. Because she was the one who had problem with whatever I do from waking up early to sleeping late at night she had problems with mostly each and every thing. But her marriage had something special for me... That was cousin my Soumya I met her after many years. I had some memories with her I can't say it was my child hood memories but definitely hers. She was 7-8 years elder than her. I remember I use to tease her showing my hair as I had longer hair then hers and she was very scared of me that she didn't even came close to me.

My First Encounter With My Polly:

Before the wedding on the same day Seema was inside sitting with Preeti and some of my cousin sister, I was bored outside serving all the baratis what they wanted my back was paining badly as we have to touch feet of every elder that comes in front of you.

"Am going inside" I said to Rajneesh my cousin brother.

"But Bhai mama will get angry" he said exclaiming my father as his mama.

"When he doesn't?" I said as I was used to of it and left the counter where I was serving gulab jamuns to all the baratis.

"What's happening dulhan?" I came inside and asked Seema.

"Nothing much this lehanga is too heavy" she said and Preeti laughed and then she continued

"You remember her?" Seema said pointing to a girl sitting next to her.

I turned around and saw a beautiful girl sitting on a red chair, she wore a simple light blue dress with lots of bangles in her hand, her hair was long, and the girls face was milky white with large dazzling chocolate brown eyes. The girl was stunningly gorgeous, like a painting of a goddess brought to life. She smiled sweetly at me, her eyes sparkling like stars flaunted on the night sky.

"Oh Teri is this Soumya?" I was shocked to see such a change in her I only remember the cute little girl with boy cut hair scared of me is now changed into such a beautiful girl.

"Yes Soumya she is" Seema said and they all laughed after seeing my expressions. I couldn't get my eyes of her she was so gorgeous.

Late that night the wedding was on and the pandit continued with his strange mantra. I saw Soumya sitting alone I went towards her. And talked for hours till the next morning.

Marriages in India are filled with ritual and celebration that continue for several days. Generally anywhere between 100 to 10,000 people attend the wedding. Often many of the attendees are unknown to the bride and the groom themselves. Wedding traditions vary across religion, caste, ethnicity, language, region, etc.

Traditional Indian weddings are generally structured into pre-wedding ceremonies, wedding day ceremonies consisting of the baraat, the varmala and the saatphere and the vidaai.

In few days all the ceremonies were done and all the relatives were gone at their place, but few of them stayed till the vidaai. The vidaai was supposed to be held from our house at the native place as the wedding was done from a wedding hall.

In few days of the wedding ceremony I and Soumya came really close to each other discussing everything about each other. Soumya and Preeti where always fond of me as they found me very interesting as I never let them get bored whenever I was around them. The time came and Seema went to her in-laws place after the vidaai ceremony. And so as everyone Soumya also went Allahabad before leaving I gave her a name and that was **"Polly"** everyone loved it specially Soumya.

I was back in Mumbai from a long vacation the first thing I was supposed to do after coming back was to meet my princess the same day I reached Mumbai.

"Where are you am waiting outside your office" I said over the phone.

"Coming just give me five minutes" Shatabdi said excitedly as she was excited to meet me after few days.

These days' couples go to famous, crowded places in first dates but they forget even though they might be adventurous with food but that doesn't mean one has to experiment with the food on the first dates. It is more important to discover and knew each other in surroundings where you are comfortable rather than knowing a new cuisine in a place where you are self-conscious.

After knowing each other and sharing or feelings with each other we had a perfect and memorable date at a beautiful Indian restaurant where the décor, lightning, music and atmosphere were exactly as she liked. We enjoyed so many dates savoring each other's company. Moreover, every date added a new shade of color to the abode of our love. We never showed our love in public places but were dedicated to each other. Our thoughts were always aligned as we believed that one rose was better than giving a bouquet of rare flowers, a gentle touch was better than public displays of affection. A smile would make each other's day and do a lot more than call each other every moment to say we loved each other.

"Shona" she said as she came running towards me and grabbed me into her arms. I could have done anything just to be in her arms. That was the best feeling I ever use to have I use to forget all my pain and worries till the time she use to hold me in her arms.

"How are you baby" I said kissing on her cheek.

"Now perfectly fine" she said with a cute smile on her face a smile like an adorable child that depicts she was happy that I was back.

"Did you bought mangoes as I said" she said with her hands inside her bag and she continued searching.

"Yes Sweetheart it's on the back seat" I said pointing towards the back seat which had two dozen of mangoes which I bought for her as she was crazy about mangoes.

"Thank u," she said and picked a mango and pealed the cover of it and then tasted it "Ammm this is yummy" she said with her eyes blinking and her lips looked as yummy as the sweetest mango in the universe.

"Let's go Vishwanand restaurant" she said.

"Why" I said as we always use to visit 'Chop King' restaurant at Vashi station.

"Arey I need to give dozen of this to my friend she is coming there" she said picking up the whole packet of mangoes.

"Ok ok madam" I said and we drove towards the restaurant near CBD Belapur bus depot which was five minutes away from her office. She gave the mangoes to her friend and then I dropped her at her place.

That night at gym I got a message from none another than my loving sister Polly.

Polly: "Hi Bhaiyya.. –Polly"

Me: "Arey Polly tu, kaisa hai beta?" (I replied as I didn't expected her message)

Polly: "Am getting so bored here ☹ how's you?"

Me: "Am Good Sweetheart, in the gym right now working out"

Polly: "Oh okay, you workout I'll message you later"

Me: "Arey that's ok we can chat no issues"

Polly: "No no you concentrate on your workout I'll message you later bye take care"

Me: "Ok keep messaging beta, bye take care"

So this was our first chat which we didn't knew that would later turned into hours of texting., During my stay at my native place while Seema's wedding Polly was my only cousin with whom I felt comfortable to share everything and so does it continued on texting, all of sudden, my sister now seems like the most important person to me. She's was an amazing girl and she deserved all the happiness in the world. Sometimes, you only realize how much a person means to you when you're apart. Well that's exactly was the situation here.

I chatted with Priyanka and Polly daily for hours while Polly was my sister Priyanka became my best friend till now, and Shatabdi my LIFE…

Those three girls were closest to me even thou I had many of the friends but the 'She Factor' took over it... A girl plays an important role in your life. Not only does she listen to you but also motivates you to achieve your goals, to face problems and resolve difficult issues. I few start describing a girl or woman; we might say many things about her but can't finish easily, because words are not enough to describe how great she is. She just needs your love and trust, respect and dedication to be with her forever.

ACT ELEVEN

Bonding With The Girls

The greatest feeling in the world is to be around with someone who wants to hold you, wants to kiss your forehead, wants to be around you, and wants to call you at night. Wants to see you smile. But I think what's better than that feeling is someone who does it all because they want to see you happy and I had three of those and luckily three of them were girls.

I was closest to Shatabdi as she was my day my night, my dark my light... Having her in my life was wonderful. She taught me how to be happy even when I had lots of problems. But she taught me as well to face the problems when I'm ready., She never questioned me why I am talking to Priyanka she knew everything as I never kept anything hidden from her. I even told Priyanka about Shatabdi and even made them talk on phone once.

Priyanka often cursed for not meeting her even thou we were such a great friends.

"You are such a jerk do you know that" Priyanka said on the call.

"Oh yes thank you I know that even Shatabdi says the same" I said I laughed.

"Oh poor Shatabdi she has to deal with this idiot daily and for the lifetime" she said and burst into laughter.

"Ha Ha Ha... Bad joke" I replied and continued "do you know where I am?"

"In my heart" she flirted as usual she use to. I often said her am the guy it's me who should flirt not you she use to say 'shut up am different' and definitely she was.

"Am in Andheri Lokhandwaala" I said.

"Oh My God Seriously" she said in a loud voice. "Yes seriously" I replied.

"Stay there and give me ten minutes I'll come and pick you up" she said as I told her the exact location where I was and surprisingly was very close to her home.

She came in next five minutes she parked her car on the other side of the road and came running towards me this was the first time I was meeting her.. She was wearing denim shorts and white t-shirt "Super Girl" written on it.

She came and hugged me and said "thank you for coming"

"I had a meeting in Andheri east I came for that not for you" I said and laughed.

"Accha then what are you doing in Andheri west kamine macchar marne aaya hai" and she slapped me on my shoulder and we both smiled.

"Come on lets go home" she said holding my hands.

"Are you mad what I'll do there, no am not coming home" I said.

"Oh hello I am not going to take your advantage relax I know you are committed" she said and dragged me towards the car and then took me at her place.

She unlocked the Dorr.

"Come in." she said and threw her handbag on the sofa.

"Thanks," I said and closed the door. Her place was beautiful and very different from other houses I had seen. It was decorated with stickers, cartoons, wind chimes and chandeliers. It looked like a house I have saw in few films.

"My sexy lady forgot her papers. Now she'll shout at me" she took a few papers and put them into cupboard.

"Who?" I asked.

"My Mom" she said.

I sat on a chair near a table which was filled up with papers and files and fruit basked. I could smell coffee in every corner of her house. "You are crazy about coffee, isn't it? I asked, standing a looking at the portrait of, I guessed, her mom and dad. She looked at me; her lips pressed together and eyes squinting, and asked, "Why" she offered me a water bottle and went into the kitchen. "This is your mom and dad portrait, right?" I asked.

She peeped from the kitchen, "Oh yes my mom and dad's twenty-third marriage anniversary, Auckland city Newzealand.

"Sugar?" she asked.

"Not too much," I replied.

We were having some conversation and the door bell.

"That would be mom" she said and stood up to open the door.

And then a not so old lady entered the room I stood up to great her.

"Hello aunty Namaste" I said.

"Mumma this is Maddy I told you naa once, my friend whose stays in..." Priyanka said as she was trying explain her mom who I was.

"Ohh ya ya I remember" she said "how's you beta? Did he have anything?" she said looking at me and then at Priyanka.

"Oh yes aunty I had coffee" I said. "Only coffee Priyanka go and order some food we'll have lunch together" she said to Priyanka

"No aunty it's late I should leave" I said and looked at Priyanka she knew what I meant to.

"Mumma he has a meeting in an hour" she said.

"Oh ok work comes first visit any other day we'll go for lunch or dinner at our restaurant" Mrs.Verma said.

"Sure aunty thank you Namaste bye Priyanka I'll see you soon" I said and moved towards the doo.

"Wait I'll drop you" Priyanka said.

"Arey nahi no need I'll manage" I said wearing my shoes

"Wait I'll come downstairs with you" she smiled and came downstairs with me.

"Thanks for this time," I smiled and said.

"My pleasure and you owe me a chocolate. Don't forget" she waved as I walked to the other side of the road and caught an auto rickshaw to Andheri station and from their train to home.

This was the first time I met Priyanka and even her mother they both were so sweet towards me why can't Shatabdi's mother be good with me. I thought in mind and in another second I got my answer,

Because she is going to be your 'Mother-in-Law' and when you re-arrange those letters it turns out into 'Women-Hitler'

From that day our friendship grew much stronger than it was I told Shatabdi about the visit at Priyanka house she was as relaxed as I expected. Her trust on me was thing which never let me to cross my line.

And talking about my sister Soumya (Polly) she got shifted from Allahabad to Gurgaon (Amity University) for her further studies we both came so close to each other after Seema's wedding we use to chat for hours I even visited Gurgaon on her birthday just remind her that she is special to me. I got to know many things about her...

She was beautiful inside and out. She was genuinely generous and kind. She was funny. She was polite but a bit naughty sometimes. She has some hidden talents too... She can sing (hilarious) she can dance (Much Hilarious) and well, she knows how to love a brother. She use to adore pretty things, such as clothes, accessories, bags... in short she loves FASHION.

My sister is pretty much the best sister you could possibly have. She knows how to be fair. She's always around when I need her. And she loves me like crazy and even I do.

I still do remember growing up with her., I use to scare her with my big eyes and hair I always taunted her as "my hair is bigger than yours" she had a Boy Cut hair back that time. She used to be a hard headed person, a naughty-girl as I use to describe her but then we didn't talked much., time passed, she's a grown up girl now an independent one.. a strong powerful girl who is sufficient to rule a community.

So basically, what I'm saying here is that my sister is the most Awesome-iest Sister ever.

ACT TWELVE

Drifting Apart

Another year passed and it was time for my elder brother Durgesh to get married, thou it was tough to convince him for the marriage as even he was in a relationship with a girl... over the years he tried his best to convince my family member for his love marriage but my family was against it because the girl was Punjabi., Even my elder sister Poonam didi pleaded in front of me to talk to Durgesh and tell him to marry the girl they want. I it did in my way, and he reacted in his way... once I even tried to convince my elder sister for my brothers love marriage but that didn't worked at all. at last after six months my brother decided to get marry to the girl my family wanted. He gave up his happiness just to raise a smile on my father's face.

He was like that from the beginning in school he scored highest rank to make my father smile, in colleague he got more than eighty percentages to make my father smile; he joined our family business just to make my father smile. All his life he made our dad proud and smile which I was never capable of and that's why the bonding between me and my father was not that good he always expected me to be like Durgesh but I never even tried. His elder son was enough to make him smile and proud which he did from childhood.

I still don't know why Indian parents are against love marriages? Didn't they know Shiva – Parvati, Krishna – Rukmani all had love marriages without even checking the horoscopes. I always believed that your first and foremost responsibility is to yourself, not to your parents not to your boyfriend/girlfriend. Choose whatever gives you happiness. You can't make others happy unless you're happy yourself. That's simple fact of life. If you feel your parents are trying to force you into a lifetime of unhappiness, you don't need to feel guilty about disappointing them.

After all the drama and all the sacrifices the day came when my brother tied his knot to a beautiful girl called Anjali. Seeing them standing on the stage only thing that came to my mind was "This is destiny from being a complete stranger they are now life partners" but it looked like they have been in love from years. They looked perfect together and why not they were made for each other. I was lost into my thoughts.

"Bhai lets goo beer thandi hojayegi" Rajneesh said while rocky was standing two bottles of beer in his hand.

"Not here lets go in my car" I said with a wink. "What will u both have, as this two bottles are for me" rocky said holding the bottles even tighter and a huge smile on his face as if he was just won the world cup.

"You can put those two into you're your ass we have another six bottles in maddy's car" Rajneesh said and gave a hi-fi to me and we burst into laughter.

Rajneesh was one of my elder cousin brothers and we were very close to each other, we always shared each and everything about our life to each other. One more major similarity between us was we both had Bengali girlfriends. Her girlfriend Manaswita Sarkar was also Bengali girl from Kolkata I met her when she came at my place with Rajneesh just before Seema's wedding. She was an amazing girl and mostly like the Bengali girls she was straight forward and a carrier oriented girl. She always said me one thing *"Because of you and Shatabdi I believe there could be real love"* and I loved it each time she said.

Unlike us rocky wasn't in a relationship he devoted his life to beers, whisky, cigarettes, and all the girls who came in her life for a short period of time. Thou he truly loved a girl in his office named Gargi Singh. Unluckily that girl left India and went to London and his love story stopped even before it could have started.

We always use to make the most of it when we three use to be together so certainly we did at Durgesh's wedding. Few days after the wedding Rajneesh went to Jharkhand where he was working with Airtel, Rocky left to his place to spend some time with his family and I came to Mumbai.

"I want to meet you now" Shatabdi called up and said.

"Baby I have just arrived, I am tiered" I said in a sleepy voice as I was tiered driving car for past twenty hours from Lucknow to Mumbai.

"You always find some excuse to ignore me" she said in an irritated voice.

"What excuse? Accha thik hai do one thing you come at my place" I said and called her at my home as no one was there from my family member it was only me who arrived from our native place.

"Ok I am coming. Bye!" she said and disconnected the call.

She arrived at my place in next twenty minutes. The door bell rang and that beautiful face arrived at my door. I opened the door and welcomed her inside she sat on sofa in my living room.

"I need to talk" she said holding the pillow kept aside on the sofa.

"Yes baby we'll talk, you want water?" I said and moved towards the kitchen.

She followed me and said "Can't you understand am talking to you", I took the water bottle from the fridge and poured it into the glass and handed it over to her and said "Haan baba bolo"

"Why you reacting so normal" she said and drank the water.

"Is there something wrong? Why shouldn't I behave normal" I said as I was confused what she was talking about.

We had few fights previously and it was quite normal as we use to have over the years.

"Will you marry me or not" she said with a sad face still standing in the kitchen I moved towards her held her hand in mine and said "Yes sweetheart why won't I? What made you think like that" I said and I kissed her hand she was into tears I hugged her I kissed her on her forehead.

Yes we had many fights during these days, I even ignored her sometimes I even said her *'we might have to spilt up'* just because of the days I saw my dad and my elder sister requesting my brother to get married to the girl of their choice. At that point of my life I thought if my brother gets married to his girlfriend I have to stay back and be with my parents to take care of them the way they did until now. Even thou now I was dam sure that my family will never accept Shatabdi as my wife. But I decided it myself it's only her whom I'll get married no matter how I do it.

"I love you" I said and came inside rest on the bed as my back was paining. She didn't replied and I said again "I said I LOVE YOU".

"I heard that, so?" she said and now she was reacting as everything was normal.

I said nothing; lying on my bed I closed my eyes for few seconds.

"I am going" she said while she was trying to wake me up. I didn't realize but I slept for almost four hours.

"Ohh what's the time?" I said with one eye closed and fighting hard to control the other one to get closed.

"Its 5:30" she said and picked her bag kept on the table in the living room.

I came to the bedrooms door and asked her "Should I drop you?" as she was opening the door.

"No I'll mange you sleep" she slammed the door and went.

I messaged her.

"Baby I told you earlier I was tired, I am sorry please ☹"

She didn't bother to reply to my message and I went on to sleep again.

Soon her birthday came. In the past four months she fought with me on every possible topic. And stayed quiet on each and every topic only thing she comes up with was 'When we are getting married' and I use to say 'Very soon just let me arrange some capital for us' she never said me why she was in a hurry to get married every time I asked her she didn't bothered replying.

Keeping every fight beside I planned to make her smile on her birthday, my friends Aabid, Neeyaz, Wasim and my cousin Rocky joined me as they wanted to meet her because they haven't met her in long while. And what's better than a birthday each of them grabbed some gifts for her and I as usual bought thirteen roses and small soft toy for her., her favorites.

"Happy Birthday sweetheart" I said over the call and planted a kiss on the phone.

"Thank you" she said with no excitement.

"What happen," I asked "Nothing" she replied.

"Am outside your house baby come" I said and stepped out of the car.

"I won't be able to come you may leave" she said in a plane voice.

"What happen? Listen am really sorry but it's your birthday don't ruin it" I almost pleaded.

"Don't be sorry, and I can't come you may leave" she said again.

I didn't said a word then and disconnected the call.

"What happen everything's ok?" Neeyaz asked me from inside the car. "Ya everything's fine, she can't come her relatives are there so her mom is not letting her go" I lied to them.

"Oh so now what?" Wasim said coming out of the car.

"Now what! What? Aabid here take this cake and go and give it to her" I said and handed the cake which I bought for her birthday celebration to over Aabid he was the guy who looked liked an emoji who had food poisoning,

"So I need to go at her home now?" Aabid asked me. "Obviously" I said and pushed him towards her building's direction. He went and came back quickly after delivering the cake at my in-laws door step. We sat in the car and were about to leave and my cell phone ranged it was Shatabdi I picked it up immediately.

"Hey sweetheart" I said with full excitement as I didn't wanted to ruin her birthday.

"Where are you" she said "Am still outside your compound about to leave what happen?" I replied.

"If you want we can meet for five minutes" she said "That's more than enough for me am waiting" I said.

She came in next ten minutes. As soon she came I hugged her and planted a kiss on her both the chicks and said "Happy Birthday Beta, Thanks for coming"

"That's ok, and thanks for the cake and the gifts" she said. Everyone wished her and then as she said 'Five Minutes' she left to her place.

ACT THIRTEEN

The Unexpected

In our ten years of relationship I and Shatabdi had billions of fight regarding each and everything. We use to scream on each other like the orangutans in the zoo love each other as purely as a mother loves her child and fight like the best friends on silly topics each and every friend of mine and hers knew about us even our family knew about us. Our love was strong enough to overcome every difficulties that life threw to us.

But form the past four months nothing was going in our favor we both had fight almost every day. Sometimes we didn't talk to each-other for few days. We never use to do that there wasn't a day when we don't use to talk. Everything was changing slowly in front of our eyes and we were ignoring it. I was busy in my work and she was busy in her.

Few days later my dad wasn't feeling well so he was admitted after few check-ups doctor said it's just because his sugar level was increased there's nothing to worry about. He was hospitalized for almost five days in the hospital near Shatabdi's house at vashi sector 9. Sixth day was the high time when my elder brother Durgesh and one of my uncle decided to move to a better hospital for better treatment as we didn't saw any improvement in dad's health.

Dad was shifted 'Sterling Wockhardt Hospital' located in sector 7 vashi itself it was quite reputed hospital in terms of everything. As soon as he was shifted there they did multiple of tests on him. And later on the doctor Sunil Kutty a Neurosurgeon called up my uncle and my elder brother to have chat with them regarding dad's situation. Soon after the chat with the doctor my uncle and my brother came up to us where I was standing in bunch with my elder sister Poonam and some of our relatives.

"There's a blood clot in dad's brain, it need to operated now" my brother said in a tensed voice as he said that my elder sister burst in tear she was the closet to my dad I could understand what she was feeling, my relatives begun to console my sister as I stood there blankly my uncle and my brother went to finish up the formalities to start the operation as soon as possible.

They came back and revealed that the doctor will be operating him tomorrow. This was just so unexpected for me even thou the doctor said there's nothing to worry about, it was depressing for me to see my dad in such pain he was able to move by himself without help of an attendant. No matter how much he use to sold me, no matter how much we are non-connected, no matter if we didn't talked for months. In the end of the day he is my dad and I could have done anything for him.

The next day afternoon doctor operated dad and it was a successful surgery, my dad was now out of danger and at that point the happiest person on the earth would have been my elder sister Poonam and why not a father is the one who looks out for the entire family. A father is his daughter's best friend, who understands her and tells her the difference between trustworthy and fake relationships. Seeing his little girl grown up is tough for every father but the best is the one who comes forward and talks to his daughter openly about everything like a friend. From putting the baby to sleep, changing her diapers and giving her baths to shaping her self-esteem, self-image and confidence, he always walks with his daughter.

Day after the surgery of my dad I decided to meet Shatabdi and take her out for a dinner and make the day special for her as we have been fighting for almost a week now and she didn't even knew about my dad's surgery. I called her

"Hello mam, how are you? still angry?" I said

"Tumse matlab, kaam kya bolo?" She said in an angry tone

"Calm down meet me after your office, okay" I said as calmly I could have.

"I don't want to meet you" she shouted

"Arey sorry naa baba I was tensed dad went thru a surgery yesterday that's why am so sorry please understand" I replied.

"What happen to papa? Is he ok now? Why didn't you said me that before?" she shot few questions repeatedly.

"All is ok now meet me in the evening ok" I said and she replied "Ok".

Her voice seem to changed, the way she was talking was something different I could understand her in and out there was something wrong she was hiding something from me.

Day evening I met her near vashi station

"What happen to dad suddenly" she asked as she was worried. I explained her whole story. And suddenly she said.

"When are we getting married" she's been asking the same question from past five – six months but this time I had an answer.

"Next year on your birthday for sure" I said with a smile.

"No marry me tomorrow itself" she said bluntly.

"Are you kidding baby" I said and laughed a bit as I taught she was kidding.

"Not at all marry me tomorrow or leave me forever" she said in a loud voice.

"Baby that's not possible, at least wait for April will get married then" I said.

"Why don't you understand my parents wants me to get married soon I can't ignore them till April" she said.

"Arey so tell them to find someone for your elder sister first, you can easily escape their taunts" I gave her a proper excuse.

"Am getting married day after tomorrow" she said.

"Whatt?" I said and she kept silent for a minute and I asked her again "What rubbish are you talking?"

"Am not talking rubbish there's a guy in our church he talked to my mom and they are okay with it" she said.

"And you?" I asked. "Yes even I said yes for the marriage" she replied without even looking into my eye.

"Are you mad, am I stupid here doing every possible things to make you happy. Arranging money so that we can live happily after our marriage and you just yes to a guy who talked to your mom and they are ok with it" I said in a loud voice as I was shocked, confused and didn't know how to react at that point.

"Even I know that guy he is a nice guy" she said

"What the fuck is that are you gone helloo are you in your senses?" I said waving my hands in front of her eyes and again she managed to ignore to look into my eyes.

"Then let's get married tomorrow" she said.

"Baby why don't you understand my dad in hospital lying on a bed and you want me to get married now? At least give me some time a month or so?" I pleaded

"so you are not going to marry me yesterday" she questioned me again.

"How can I, I told you about my dad still you want this?" I replied.

"Ok, well am leaving now you better forget me and start your life on a good note again, and please don't try to contact me again bye" she said and begun to move.

"What is this don't be stupid we love each other why you doing this" I said as I walked behind her.

"No we don't, at least I don't love u... Now will you please stop following me?" she said in so ease that I froze their itself I couldn't believe she said that I didn't moved from their and saw her catching a rickshaw and disappearing from my sight I was never been so scared of losing something in my entire life, then again noting in my life ever meant as much to as she did.

I messaged her that night itself.

"Baby please understand I love you give me some time please☹" and then she replied after an hour.

"Please don't message me am engaged" I was stunned shocked I didn't had anything to say her I messaged her called again and again but she didn't responded to any of my calls. I was bit angry I thought I should give her sometime and decided not to message or call her for a day or two.

Those two days were like hell to me I felt so bad that I didn't even tell my closet friends. When everyone was thinking I am fine because I was smiling, but that thing was killing me. And the worst part was that, that no one knew about it, I didn't said anyone about it because they won't understand.

After two days I called her again but her phone was switched off. I tried her second number that said not reachable. I was confused what would have happened lot of things were going in mind did she really moved on? Is she really engaged? Was she upset with me? If yes then why? And many questions were in my head but I didn't have answer of any of those.

I decided to go at her place and I went there with one of my friend Shaan standing outside her society we were confused should I go directly or should we call any of her family members. And then we decided to call first I had her mother's number I gave it to Shaan he called her.

"Hello can I talk to Shatabdi" he said normally

"She went for honeymoon with his husband, don't call again" her mother replied and disconnected the call.

She knew I would try to reach up to her daughter she was ready for an answer. An answer which was hurting me so badly. I wanted to meet her anyhow at any cost. As her mother was not ready to reveal the truth if that was the truth what she said I was not in a mood to believe it. I called up my childhood friend peter, yes the one who paired us together I felt he is the one who'll fix this. And in the next fifteen minutes he was there standing next to me. That's the beautiful thing about friends they are always there when you need them we didn't had t a word in past six months but still he was there for me just because I was sad. I explained him all the situation from the beginning he then called up one of my another childhood friend Raj and then both of them decided to go at her home.

They went and came back in less than a five minutes and peter said.

"Her elder sister Sharbani opened the door slightly and as I asked is Shatabdi there she said she is out of India for her honeymoon and slammed the door in front of us"

I didn't said a word and stood there quietly with tears in my eyes, peter came up to me and said "don't worry brother we'll find her she can't hide from us and as soon as we find her we'll kidnap her" with a wink.

I smiled and told them that tomorrow is Sunday Shatabdi use to visit church every Sunday so if she is inside the house she'll surely go to church next morning. And we decided to be around her house from morning so that we don't miss a chance to talk to her. Peter and raj said they'll come in the morning at 7am as we didn't knew at what time she'll come out so I decided to spend the night in car the near her building.

All night I only thought about our journey thru the years. We had some beautiful memories together all the night the hardest decision to take was to walk away or try harder because at it is said the moment you feel like you have to prove your worth to someone is the moment you need to walk away from them. But I choose to try harder just because I wasn't ready to give up on my relationship even if I was the only one holding it. She was my dream I was willing to risk everything for her.

Next day morning peter came at 8am and raj at 9am we were sitting at the back gate of her society and then I saw a girl going out towards the main gate of their building. I could have recognized that girl even if my eyes were closed it was Shatabdi.

"There she is" I said pointing towards her and peter had a look and said "Sharbani the bitch am not gonna leave her first let's talk to Shatabdi Start the car" as we sat inside the car I saw her mother following her from her back, so we decided just to follow her and wait for the right moment .

Her mother and she got into a rickshaw and we followed them as they went inside the "Meghalaya House" near vashi station and we waited for almost four hours till she came out but this time she was surrounded by her mother and her aunty as well.

We stood and saw from a distance when a white Santro car came to pick them up we didn't knew who he is, I taught it might be her aunt's son who usually use to come with different car to pick them up and then again we followed them her mother got down at vashi but Shatabdi was still in the car so we followed them again we decided we'll stop her once the right moment come but it didn't went our way the car went inside another society in which her aunty use to stay in Kopar Khairne.

We taught we missed the chance to confront Shatabdi. But then peter's phone rang and it was Shatabdi. She called peter from her aunt's number we taught she didn't saw us but she did.

Peter received the call, only thing I could hear was what peter saying, he said many things such as "where are you? / Why you avoiding us? Ok at least talk to Maddy once? / "and then he kept the phone and said "she doesn't wants to meet any of us and says am married you all stay away from me & stop following me"

"She can't do that peter please talk to her she is just angry tell her to meet me once" I pleaded in front of peter.

"Ok wait I'll call her again on the same number" he said patting my shoulder. He called her again and this time she got ready to meet peter, she didn't wanted to face me and I still didn't knew why.

Peter called her again and convinced her to meet him she still didn't wanted to meet me. As peter and raj were walking away to meet Shatabdi I just said "Please make her understand" to them and cried peter moved forward to me hugged me and said don't worry and they went.

The time while I was waiting for peter and raj to come back I was thinking about what went wrong I gave my all to our relationship but still what went wrong? Was I the culprit of my love story? And many more questions were going thru my mind I didn't even had a chance to face her and make her realize that I loved her so much., Those moments were worst moment in my life when I was able to see my whole world was falling apart and all I can do was stare blankly.

After some time peter and raj came back I ran towards them the first thing peter said was "She is changed totally changed you better forget her and move on" he said putting his hand on my shoulder.

"But what did she said" I said grabbing peter's choler.

"She said u didn't gave her time and was not ready to get married to her that's why she moved on, she was shouting on us like a mad professor we couldn't say anything after that" he said and looked down.

I was blank I didn't had anything to say either I just started crying in the middle of the road I fell on my knees and cried harder. When you fall in love its intoxicating. And for a little while you feel like you've actually become one with the other person. Merged souls, and so on. You think you'll never be lonely again. Only it doesn't last and soon you realize you can only get so close, and you end up brutally disappointed, more alone than ever, because the illusion- the hope you'd held on to all those years- has been shattered.

Raj held my shoulder and made me stand I was still crying I hugged him and said "If I knew where I went wrong I'd turn the world around to make it right, please raj I want to talk to her just once please" he said nothing just held me in his arms.

Peter came up to me with a bottle of water and said "Here wash your face and lets go there point crying for someone who doesn't give a shit about you"

"But you know how much I love her and this isn't a reason that I didn't gave her time yes I wasn't able to give her time in the past month just because my dad was in hospital I had to look after him but I was always there for her whenever she needed me financially, emotionally, physically I was always there" I said controlling on my tears.

"When you give someone the leading role in the story of your life and they turn it down, it's time to do a rewrite" peter said.

"Rewrite?? I can't even close this chapter brother" I said wiping my tears and continued "Anyways you guys leave thanks for all this" I said and moved towards my car.

"Where are you going?" raj asked from behind.

"Somewhere in peace" I said and sat inside the car and accelerated it.

My heart was crying and it was the worst type of crying. The silent one. The one when nobody can listen you. The one when you feel it in your throat, and your eyes become blurry from tears. The one where you want to scream. The one where you have to hold your breath and grab your stomach to keep quiet. The one where you can't breathe anymore. The one when you realize the person that meant the most to you, Is Gone.

I stopped my car at the old Vashi Bridge I didn't know what was going thru my mind I just wanted to end my life right over there I felt like I belong no were in the world., It was fucking terrifying that no matter how many promises they made, no matter how long you've been together, someone can get up and walk out of your life without a second thought and you have to carry on living because the world doesn't stop any of us.

I got out of my car wiping my tears. Standing at the edge of the bridge I thought how much time it'll take to finish my life, it was just a matter of second. I felt like I don't have any choices left my phone ranged and it was Priyanka I ignored the call thrice but she repeatedly called me for fourth time and as soon I received it.

"What is wrong with you why can't you receive my call at first ring?" she shouted as she was irritated by calling me four times in a row.

I said nothing standing at the edge of the bridge wiping my tears planning to finish my life over there.

"Hello sir am talking to you" she said again louder this time.

"Ya am sorry" I tried to say that in a normal tone so that she won't recognize I was crying but she knew me very well.

"What happen are you crying" She said.

"No rey baba just not feeling well" I said with a sniff.

"Do you think am stupid?" she said

"I don't think I know you are" I acted as everything was fine.

"Swear on me and say everything's ok" she asked me again.

It hurts when you go through something that kills you inside but you have to act like it doesn't affect you at all. I was doing the same from time she called me but at last I broke into tears.

"Hey Maddy what happen will you tell me please, why are you crying?" She said in a worried tone.

I was crying like a little baby who is been lost in the crowd trying to control on my tears I said

"She got married to someone else"

"What the fuck? But it was all well back a month ago when we had a word" she said.

Then I told her the whole story that happen between us. The little fight we had between us, the argument regarding marrying her tomorrow itself. Everything.

And I burst into tears again. Sometimes there's no huge fight that marks the end of a relationship. No falling out, no major disagreement. Sometimes it just falls apart for no good reason. Distance, New relationships, Priorities. Somehow these things can become more important than your connection, they shouldn't but they do.

"Where are you? I want to meet you now" she said, she was worried for me.

"I want to meet Shatabdi, I want to know the reason what I did wrong I still don't believe she can marry someone else" I said and cried again.

"Listen to me first you need to meet me you get it am coming, where are you just tell me we'll together go and meet her" she said

"I don't want to meet anyone sorry bye" I said and disconnected the call.

As soon as I disconnected Priyanka's call I got a call from my elder brother.

"Where are you" he shouted form the other end.

"In Vashi, what happen?"I replied.

"Shatabdi's mother called me now, why don't you leave her alone she is married now, why you following her" he shouted again.

Oh the devil the women who once promised me that she will never let me take her daughter proved her point and I was standing like loser on the edge of a bridge trying to take my own life. I said nothing to my brother just said "Ok I won't" and disconnected the call.

As I disconnected the call my cell phone beeped and flashed an msg.

It was from Priyanka and it said.

"Sometimes the people you want as part of your story are only meant to be a chapter. Please don't do anything wrong we love you"

When it happens, you won't want to believe it. You'll take their word for it when they said "It's Over" you'll make excuses for them, put your ringer on extra loud in case they call. But you'll still feel the change. In life it's given that you will lose people. People will flow in and out like curtains through an open window, sometimes for no reason at all. But losing someone important to you will feel like end of the life every single time, and you'll never see it coming.

ACT FOURTEEN

Without Her

After my breakup. Or the end of a beautiful relationship with Shatabdi, my personality changed. People around me started to call me Devdas, Aashiq and many more such name, I would sit with my friends but didn't talked at all. Initially, they tried to cheer me up. They gave me copies of adult magazines and arranged booze parties to help me get over Shatabdi. However just like their earlier advice, their break-up cures were useless too. The only thing that somewhat was my sister Soumya, every time of thought of her I use to call Soumya and talk to her about random things, this use to temporarily cure my heartache,

I miss her in my days; I miss her in my nights. I miss her every moment of my life. . .

Night hit me the hardest. I couldn't sleep. I wished I had a time machine to undo my mistakes if it were any. I didn't want a time machine to predict cricket match scores or buy cheap property. I only wanted to spend some time with her. I was bound by my stars to live a lonely life. Without her, I felt so alone. Though the fact is that it's just *she* who is gone and everything else was the same. But this 'everything else' is nothing to me...

It was almost 5-6 months she got married to someone else, but I wasn't ready to believe it. Every one said me to move on but I always wanted to talk to her once, just once I wanted to know what went wrong what I didn't do to make her happy. I Tried hell lot of things to get in touch with her just one last time to know what made her to took such a big step that's all I wanted. Losing her was hard enough, but I didn't wanted to go on knowing I mean absolutely nothing to her.

I started living alone and isolated, when my friends talked to me, I started shouting at them. My friendship went in the wrong way and I lost most of my friends. Nobody wanted to talk to me because nobody knew anything. If you're mad for something, it comes to you for sure. I had faith in my love that someday she'd come back in my life. She was nowhere on G-mail, Facebook or any other social media. I called her on number that didn't exist anymore. I tried all her numbers but no use. I was helpless. I even requested her friend Radhika to visit her place and talk to her, she even did so but Shatabdi refused to meet her and I was left unanswered again. Many of my friends and Radhika told me to move on because they couldn't see my pain. However, I never wanted to move on. I didn't want to be the part of the crowd where people love and forget. I loved once and I had to live once.

Talking about Priyanka and our friendship

The best part about Priyanka and me was that she was like a girlfriend, but a non-fussy and a non-sexual one, which meant no possessiveness, no jealousy and no obligations. But she was always there when I needed her. She was so cute and caring, almost like a mini-mom, and that's why I always thought that Priyanka is the sweetest girl to be with she anyway treated me like her lost kid. After my breakup she tried many times to meet me but every time I declined to meet her at times her caring nature confused me her respect for me and the way she supported me in my difficult situations made me wonder if she loved me thou I was quite sure about it, friendship had a very difficult meaning for her and that was, in fact more pleasant and truer that the love.

"I want to meet you today please" Priyanka said on the call.

It's was almost five months since Shatabdi broke up with me and since then I was living in a trauma. I was now not worried about my looks, my beard took over my face as the grasses took over an abandon place. I looked like a south Indian movie villain who never did a single good thing in life.

"Today not possible" I said her same thing which I repeated for last five months.

"You have been saying the same thing again and again, just listen to me Mr.Pandey if you don't meet me today I won't meet you ever" she said rudely.

"Okay baba where are you?" I said as I thought it was high time now.

"Am at home now leaving for Bandra meet me at CCD of bandstand at 3:00PM sharp get it" she said loudly but she was happy that I agreed to meet her.

"Okay my lord" I said and hung up the call and left the house as it was already 2:00PM.

I was late so buying chocolates was the best options to save myself from her scolding.

I was waiting for an auto rickshaw at Bandra station when my cell phone vibrated. You should never argue with girls or women when they are waiting for you because they haven't been created to wait, they have been made to be pampered.

"Do you wear a wrist watch?" Priyanka asked over the phone.

"Yes, I do but forgot to wear it" I knew what she was trying to do.

"Someone promised to meet me today, I think he forgot" she said.

"Someone is on the way, reaching there in ten minutes. I have something for you" the auto rickshaw was moving at a snail's pace in heavy traffic.

"That chocolate idea is not going to work, you are thirty minutes late" girls all over world will remain the same always sweet and spicy.

"I need your mercy, my lord. Just give me five minutes" I replied teasingly to make her smile.

"Shut up and come soon" the driver increased the volume of the song and looked at me in the front mirror and smiled. He accelerated wheeled towards Bandra west and dropped me in front of CCD.

Sitting alone in the corner, holding a glass of cold coffee with a straw in the corner of her mouth, she was reading a novel and just turned the last page when I entered CCD. A hair band in her silky hair made her look even more charming. She never wore heavy jewellery, bright hued lipsticks or kohl. Minimal make-up and just small diamond earrings made her so beautiful.

"When will you stop looking so gorgeous?" I said sitting by her side.

"Hey!" she looked at me, gave a smile and added, "How are you?"

"I'm good. You didn't answer. When will you stop looking so gorgeous?" I said

"Never" she smiled, placing a bookmark and keeping the book aside. "By the way, hot girls have coffee and smoking hot girls read books with coffee" she laughed out loud.

"Yes, I know, sorry for being late" I said

"It's okay. You would be dead if you had forgotten"

"I know this doesn't work every time but there was no other way to save myself" we both laughed as I gave her the chocolate. We were meeting after a long time but nothing had changed. We spent more than an hour talking about random things.

"So what do you do after work, when do you reach home?" she asked.

"Firstly, I never call it home. That is just a place where I live I don't know. I usually don't map out my timings" I said.

She looked around here and there and said "you go back to your place, work hard, plan things for the next day, have your dinner, watch TV, unlock your phone, look at her old photograph, feel bad, shed tears, shout alone and sleep with your wet pillow. Where is the life?" I didn't answer as those questions didn't have any answers.

"Think about it till I get a coffee for you" she said and stood up. The café guy was giving us a questioning looks as we were just talking and hadn't ordered much.

"Hey, you sit, I'll get it. You girls are precious, I can't make you slave" I joked

"Oh please! Sit down; I don't believe in that and my friendship demands no formalities. I'll be right back" she was smiling but I could see she was tensed that I was not looking well. Life seems precious when you start liking those peoples. Firstly Polly came to my mind and the she. She always made me smile and feel happy. Thinking these sweet and sour thoughts, as usual my mind again thought something that it was not allowed to think...

I was lost in my thoughts. "Hello!" she waved her hand in front of my face. I came out from my dreams. "NO! Nothing, thanks"

I held the glass of cappuccino.

"So ... did you think about it?" she asked, girls are girls they don't speak much but their body language speaks a lot about their feelings- she was hurt.

"Well leave it" she smiled. I couldn't answer her previous question but I was still stuck on few others.

Do people really meet again? Do we find that person for whom we live our whole life? Is it all about destiny? Will Shatabdi return to my life?

With a few sips of coffee remaining in our cups, Priyanka touched my hand. I ignored it the first time but the way she looked at me clarified many things. She liked me but since when, I didn't know. I also liked her, not because she was pretty, intelligent and a complete girl but because she was a very good person by heart.

I held her hands in mine and asked her, "Do you love me?"

She was shocked and surprised but somewhere a smile reflected on her face. Girls don't walk around wearing their hearts on their sleeves, they take time. She took time to reply and then said,

"Yes, I do" she said

Her eyes met mine. She ran her fingers in her hair and was very nervous.

"That's great. I'm so lucky. Let's go get married and run away from this world what do you say?"

She had never expected these words from me. She released her hand and said, "But You Love Shatabdi"

"If you know this then why these feeling for me? Can't we be friends? I don't want to lose you because I've already lost many. It is true that I like you a lot as my good friend we can't be life partners. I just wanted to clarify that, and I respect you and your feelings" I said.

She nodded, took my hand and kissed it. "You are a stupid but a good friend and yes, a mad lover. Just take care of yourself. Don't curb the spark within you. I'm here always with you"

We both walked out of the café and started walking along the road.

"Why don't we hire a direct taxi to your place?" I asked her. She slowed her steps and looked at me with a cute smile on her face.

"You don't like walking along the sea? Don't you like it when the waves touch your legs and try to hold your waist each time? Don't you like it" She bent and folded her denims till her knees. She came right up to the waves. I didn't speak but managed my steps with hers and tried to feel the pleasurable touch of waves.

"I want to smile, I want to laugh, I want to feel, I want to be happy, I want to live in these moments... but for whom?" I said in a low tone.

"Of course, for yourself, you have live for yourself. Nobody lives for others" she said. I took a small pebble and threw it in the sea with great force. I could not say anything after that.

"Never blame yourself. Never blame others. Good days give happiness and bad days make you mature and experienced. Good can be better but best is always the best" she said and winked.

"Oh is it" I laughed.

"Why are you hurting yourself, your family, your friends and your life?" she shouted, holding my hands in front of many people around us.

"I'm sorry, I didn't mean it but look, till when you are going to wait for her?" she said

"Till the day my hearts hates her, I'll wait for her, I loved her truly, and I will wait for her. Look at the sea... it has nothing special in it but calls us to come here every day and we feel peaceful when we are here. It holds numberless precious things in its embrace in the same way as I have those precious feelings and love for her. No matter when but she has to come; she has to give me one reason for leaving me alone..."

She smiled, patted me on my back and gave me tight hug and we moved on and got an auto rickshaw to her place.

"Come up Mumma wanted to meet you" She said as we reached Lokhandwaala Andheri.

"No you go I'll leave form here its 8 o'clock I'll be late" I said.

"Don't act like a kid" she said and held to take me with her.

As we reached her place the house which looked like I have seen in few films.

"Have a seat, Mumma is on the way she texted me" she said and went inside the kitchen.

"Water or soft drink?" she shouted from inside, as I stood up and went inside the kitchen.

"Ah let's see what you have in your fridge" I said opening the fridge.

"By the way, I can help you" she said.

"I'm not suffering from any disease. Help for what?" I asked as I took out the juice can from the fridge.

"Why don't you move on, Maddy? Have you ever looked at yourself? You have many reasons to be happy. You're talented, you're hard working and you have a cute smile. Yes, you have a cute smile." she repeated it to make me smile

"There are many things in life that we can't change. There are few people in life that we can't forget. It's tough to move on" I said, putting those can on the shelf next to me.

"And you know what; you're a complete package of romance. You can try even on me! If you can impress me, you can take advantage of me. I'm a rich girl" she smiled and then blinked her eyes. A smile tells the truth and a smile with blinks says many things. I laughed.

"Advantage?" I laughed again. "This is not a game for me to take advantage. Yes you are a rich girl but I can't lose my best friend who is priceless'" I pinched her on her nose. She looked at me like a small girl looking at her father. We both knew each other, believed strongly in each other.

She didn't say anything further, but simply stepped closer towards me with her arms wide open. I was a split second away from witnessing something beautiful. It wasn't going to be for the first time but it was going to be after so long time.

She came like a breeze and wrapper me in her arms. I felt her and I felt her feeling me. She held me tight and rested her face on my left shoulder. Her innocent hug cleared every thought from my mind, leaving me absolutely clam...

After a long time I was in a woman's arms. That moment was as if . . . as if life had suddenly fuelled back into me, as if it had rained again after a decade... it felt like the first sunrise after thousands of moonless dark nights, like the first bite of food after a hundred days of hunger.

I felt satisfied.

Tears ran down my face as I rested my face on her shoulder, she sensed that but didn't say anything, instead she gripped me tight and whispered in my ears, **"You are a sweetheart. You deserve happiness."**

I rested my head for a while on her shoulder and I gripped her tightly.

When I opened my eyes she moved her face back and looked right into my eyes. She wiped away the tears from my face. I smiled back and I hugged her again. I was happy. I don't know for how long we were there in her kitchen holding each other in our arms, leaning against the fridge. I guess until my empty heart got filled in the shower of pleasure and warmth.

Some time you are not sure how happiness can again slip into your life.

Now everything was changing slowly. Life was like an oil lamp, though I was glowing, I was burning form inside. People congratulated me on my small successes but I had lost the real subject of life that was love.

And I'll tell you what this loneliness feels like, what it feels like to live a life without the person you loved more than anything or anyone else in the world.

Recalling something about her, you happen to laugh and in no time, sometimes even as you laugh, you taste your own tears.

The more you want to avoid romance around you, the more you will find it. It will torture you. You will see couple kissing and hugging each other, resting their head on each other's shoulders. You will see them everywhere, even in the movie halls where you'll want to spend a few hours in darkness. You will find a pair sitting next to you, doing all that you, sometime in the past, did with your beloved. You will feel the pain, your heart will bleed. And, very calmly, you will walk pretending you didn't see anything.

Your friends will talk about yet another chick. But all the good-looking girls on this planet will fail to attract you. Nothing excites you, even your sexual desires go into hibernation. While working-out in the gym, you will try to lift the heaviest weights. Later, standing under the shower, you will cry hard but nobody will hear you. The splashing of the shower will mask the sound of your sobbing.

You will search for and continue anything that can erase your memory.

And, believe me; your life will appear worse than death.

Everything that brought a smile to my face had now started torturing me. At times, I felt like a drug addict who badly needs his next hit. But at least an addict has his drugs... I felt suffocated as if something was stopping my breath. As if something was choking my soul...

I got scared of things, I don't know what they were, but they wouldn't let me sleep. I use to stare at the fan rotating above me for hours and hours...

If ever I fell asleep, I would wake to nightmares, screaming. The time was always 4 am.

I still didn't gave up on the hope that she'll be back in my life I still was trying to get her back in my life even thou she was married the only question remained unanswered was why she did it? What was the reason behind it... many of my friends said it would be because she fell in love with that other guy or her mother did something supernatural to her even I believed this things at some point but my heart wasn't ready for it... it just said "talk to her once" and I kept trying. And at last I got a chance to talk to her.

It was almost a year from the day of the breakup it took me time to know where she lives now and at last I figured it out she lived in CBD Belapur. The place where her first office was located again I decided to meet her when she'll be leaving for her church prayer on Sunday. Akbar my gym buddy was there with me, he supported me in all the possible ways he could, it was because he knew love hurts like this.

We decided to wait outside of the building in the car. We were waiting for her to come I thought of many things I'll say to her when I get to talk to her I wanted to tell her how much I love her, I wanted to make her see there are a million reasons why she should stay with me.

I was lost in my dreams suddenly Akbar said "Brother is that Shatabdi"

"Oh yes she is" I said as I was seeing her after almost a year. People who are meant to be together find their ways back, they may take a few detours, but they're never lost, I thought in my mind.

"GO talk to her" Akbar said to me.

"No not now I don't want to create a scene over here" I said and we followed her as she got into an auto rickshaw and moved towards the Palm Beach road.

As the rickshaw stopped at the first traffic light near the NRI Complex, even we stopped as we were three cars behind her rickshaw.

"Bro now you have to go you won't get another chance" Akbar said to me.

I didn't said anything to Akbar and just got down from the car and moved towards the auto rickshaw she was in. My heart was pumping at double rate, my legs were shivering, I was scared to face her I don't know why but I was. I just wanted to go there and hold her in my arms and say *'I love you please don't leave like this'* I saw the traffic light meter it showed 113 seconds remaining. I knew I had 113 Seconds to get my answer.

I reached to the auto and saw her sitting inside on the back seat she looked at me and I was lost in her again she wasn't the same Shatabdi she used to be, she was totally changed she looked upset her eyes were puffy below her eyes she had the dark circles as if she has cried all the night her shoulder looked like carrying heavy weights and lips were dried I wanted to hug her there itself and say *'everything's going to be ok'* I regained my senses as the traffic meter displayed 70 seconds left. As soon I could have said anything she saw me and didn't react at all. It killed me. If she had come forward and slapped me or yelled, I would have been okay. However, she looked right through me, as if I didn't exist and then shouted on me. "What are you doing here?"

Tears rolled downed my cheeks and I said "Can I please talk to you for five minutes please?"

"No leave me alone" she screamed and cried like a baby. I wonder if she was crying for me, she tried to hide her face behind her big bag she sniffed wiped her tears which again rolled down on her cheeks and she said again "Please don't disturb me leave me alone"

The traffic signal was green now her auto moved ahead with her, I was numb, broken, shattered, and I stood there looking at her rickshaw speeding up in the Palm Beach road disappearing from my view. She walked away like it was nothing. Like we were nothing. Like I was nothing...

Everything else was gone with her, my dreams, my happiness, my smiles, my future and a lot more. I had changed a lot. I was a guy who always had fun with my friends but now my friends had started saying, "what happened Maddy, are you okay?"

I just showed them my fake smile now. I had learnt to wear fake smile but it was tough and painful. Whenever I tried to be happy and smile, I remembered all those happy moment with Shatabdi, missed her a lot and felt like crying. I stopped to pick calls and when my sister Polly called me, I washed my face so she couldn't understand that I had been crying.

When she asked me, "what happened Bhaiyya, are you crying?"

ACT FIFTEEN

Moving Away

Watching people leave is hard. But it's harder remembering that time when they promised they wouldn't.

Winter had gone in her romantic memories, summer had gone with dry days and now rains had come. It was early June when clouds started romancing around but rains were still waiting to hug Mumbai. Every weekend I used to come at the marine drive sit on the seaside after work. There was special bond that I could feel with those waves. The sky was clear and blue when I left form my dad's office in the morning. I carried an umbrella without any reasons because rains had stepped in at some other places in the state of Maharashtra. I had a special love for the rain as it washes out everything.

I remembered something, something that already had changed everything in my life. I remembered when I and Shatabdi were standing at the vashi station under the umbrella that night, she asked for an ice cream, and next morning we were both coughing but without any regrets as we had enjoyed together. Love seems so beautiful when you live together and love together for almost the whole life.

A romantic couple crossed me as they threw their umbrella and walked away into the rain. They looked like birds flying in an open sky with love and passion. I stopped a couple of times along the way to take in the beautiful views of the skyline, the sea, the beach, couples, friends, families. And me... ALONE.

The only way to cover my pain and survive was to keep smiling, find ways to cheer myself up and laugh out loud, this made me who I was. Restricting me from doing this felt like living in the desert all alone and killing myself slowly. Sometimes we want nothing more than to forget someone because the memory of them hurts us now, for whatever reason a person who used to make us smile doesn't anymore, maybe because they aren't around anymore and the memories of them remind us of that. What I've come to realize though is for all the people I wanted to forget about but couldn't was for a reason. To ensure the lesson she taught me was never forgotten. So when it comes down it for better or for worse, I'll never forget the ones even if they have hurt me, but now I don't think I'd want to.

As I was sitting at the promenade I got a call from Priyanka.

"Hey my handsome! Where are you?" she said

"Marine drive" I replied.

"Marine drive" she repeated and then continued "what are you doing there?"

"Aise hi time pass! Wanna join?" I asked

"Am not joining you, you are going to join us in next one hour" she ordered.

"And may I ask where are we going? And us? Who else?" I said.

"Arey baba its me and Sonam my friend and we are going rude lounge Bandra so tell me you coming here to pick us up or we're meeting directly at the venue?" she explained me.

"I'll meet you in Bandra" I said

"Ok so meet us at Bandra station bye see you soon" she said and hung up the call.

I reached Bandra station in next 45minutes and saw Priyanka and Sonam waiting for me near the juice corner I stopped the car in front of them and they quickly got into the car. And then we reached Rude Lounge in Bandra west. As I parked the car they waited for me at the gate.

"Be ready to rock sweetheart" Priyanka teased me, entering the gate. Sonam smiled and I followed her. Rude Lounge was in Bandra West. It had a great menu consisting of classics American fare including burgers, sandwiches and salads, waiting to awake your taste buds, while a counter also represented local flavor, consisting of favorites like chicken kebab and more. We all took our place just in front of the bar.

Unexpectedly, I was reminded of how when Shatabdi and I were together, we were always on the lookout for a decent place, less noisy and romantic... I smiled emotionally remembering those moments. We always preferred a place where we could talk and get to know each other than noisy, flashy places on initial dates.

"Hey. I want one vodka, may I?" Priyanka asked pointing to the bartender. It's very difficult to manage a girl when she is drunk. She can pull you into the worst situations, so I had one answer:

"I have the best answer for you and that is a big NO," I said and pinched her softly on the cheeks.

"Please. Even I don't have an idea as to when I'd be coming here again. Just one please, please…" she requested like an adamant child almost pleading by the end of it.

"Yes, what's the big deal? Even as children we all had Dr Brandy. Isn't it? Priyanka said while Sonam was looking at us.

"Okay, then I'll tell aunty to give you Dr Brandy once we reach home, but as of now, NO, you can't drink. We have to reach home before 11:00 pm else your mom will file a police complaint against me. Hope you understand. We'll try this next time for sure. Okay?" I said in a serious tone to Priyanka.

"If you won't allow me, then I'll tell my mom that you took advantage of us girls tonight" she said gravely.

"Good try… I still can't allow you sweetie" I teased her.

"So mean you are." But she remained seated, holding a glass rolling the ice cubes in it.

The waiter served our food, and I tried to keep her busy with the food and conversation so that she couldn't repeat that again.

"How's she?" Priyanka had said with a bite of the French fries Sonam did the same.

"Who?" I asked, looking around. A bouncer, a bulky black man caught my eye.

"That girl in ultra mini skirt with 34-24-32" Priyanka widened her eyes and slowly turned to the girl who was wearing a whit T-Shirt that had a few abstract drawing across the chest with these words at the bottom- 'What you looking at?' Her hair looked like someone had cut it with garden shears but she had the perfect curves.

"Should I talk to her for you?" Sonam said, curling a tendril of hair around her finger and sipping a glass of strawberry shake. I scoffed and growled at the same time.

"Okay. No problem" she smirked and took a small sip of lemonade from Priyanka glass. The music became louder, and the air inside became hazier. All waiters came together and started dancing, standing on the small platform which separated the café in the bar from the other area. I had heard about the evening dance of Rude Lounge but it was a lot of fun to watch their sing-song movements. Sonam clapped down on the table in excitement. The smoke in the café was swirling around. Chilling time, ice cool glasses in hands, some with beer, some with soft drinks and only one with melting cubes of ice (mine).

"Happy?" turning her eyes like a juggler while snapping her fingers, Priyanka asked me. She knew about the phase I had gone through in past few months.

"For what?" I questioned, finishing the last pieces of French fries from the plate.

"Are you not happy being here after a long time?" Priyanka asked, expecting a reply in the affirmative.

"Off course I am thanks a lot for this" I pinched her on her nose. I never wanted to leave her. After losing almost everything. I had only few things in my life- my best friend Priyanka…

My wristwatch said it was 11:05 pm. I had to reach before 11:00.

"Let's go guys," I said, having a sip of water.

Priyanka interrupted in between, "just one last shot of vodka"

"What's that?" I asked her. Before I could confirm that she was having vodka, she had emptied the glass.

"When did you order this? Are you crazy?" I almost shouted at her.

"I'm sorry for that but I wanted to have just one peg," she sounded completely drunk.

"What sorry, Priyanka?" I shouted.

"I have lost control over myself, please give me your hand and help me stand up" she said. She swung to the other side. I stood up and held her, putting my hands on her shoulders and came out of the café. Everybody around was staring at us, especially her and me, the way I held her and she hung on me. "You know, you're my best friend, only you can get me out of this" she laughed. I held her hand; drunken Priyanka was out of her senses.

A guy was staring at us and had been noticing us for quite some time. He came up to us and said, "May I help you?"

"No. we're good. Thanks. I can manage" I placed my jacket upon her shoulder and held her. He went away. Sonam was scared to go home

"It is 11:15 pm aunty had already called her twice and mom had called me just ten minutes back" Sonam said in a low voice.

This was going to be a big mess and I regretted coming here.

"We'll have to sleep on the road in this winter" I answered in anger.

"I don't want to go, I don't want to go" she sang

"Now stop it, Priyanka, control yourself" Sonam held her waist and moved ahead.

Getting these girls home safely was a huge task for me. The streets were dark and deserted. The few street lights that were on were no better those years old oil lamps in the dense fog.

"Let's go now. Enough fun for the day" Priyanka said and started laughing.

She gave a childish smile, very similar like a kid who'll give her mother after stealing jam from the kitchen.

"Sorry, I just wanted us to have fun and make this day memorable for us. Hope you won't forget..." she said, holding her ears in a gesture of asking for forgiveness.

She was not drunk. She had just pulled a prank on me.

"I'll kill you" I tried to catch her. She laughed like the evil.

"How can I do this without your permission?" she said. I was angry but her craziness made me smile.

"Now we're getting late, let's go" I opened the door of my car and made them sit inside...

"Yup lets go dad is not well mom texted me just now" Priyanka said

"Why what happen suddenly" I asked

"I don't know I just got a text from Mumma" she said showing her phone's screen towards me. Which displayed

"Come home Soon beta dad is not well he's asking about you?"

"Ok don't worry It'll take 15 minutes to reach at your place" I said and accelerated the car and Dropped them at their respective places and I returned back home.

Days were passing by without her I missed her each and every day I wanted her to be with be nights were toughest for me I loved to sleep but now I started hating nights and my bed. Suddenly I used to wake up in the night missing her, and would start crying. SMILE, it seemed I just forgot how to do that. Every day I cried, looking here and there in the empty room, walked and again come to my bed, I would start crying but nobody was there to listen to me and then I ended up keeping pillow on my head and spending nights like that just cried looking at the photographs. Sometimes I tried to hate them to feel better but I couldn't. I just shouted alone in the room. Hit myself to the walls and slept just with my tears and wet pillow. I used to walk at 3o'clock in the night as I felt I am alone in the world and lonely. I logged on my computer to see her photograph early in the morning and checked mails expecting that someday she'll mail me a voice mail to give me surprise but I forgot, nobody was missing me, nobody was there to even look at me.

I use to call Priyanka at nights at 3:00 AM she always use to entertain me in the middle of the night. Every time I called her she uses to say "Again you've called me in the middle of the night. Do one thing, come marry me and be with me forever. Can't you see me happy?" in an unclear voice. Most of the times I use to wake her up from her sleep and talk to her about random things and end up talking about Shatabdi she never interrupted me because she knew what I was going thru.

It was the last week of June Priyanka's dad wasn't really well so he was been admitted in hospital for regular chest pain. Those are the times when your friends need you the most. And as her best friend I was always there for her I regularly visited the hospital to take a look if everything was fine.

It was Thursday morning when I was on my way to office I got a call from Priyanka's number when I was half way down I stopped my car aside and received her call as soon I picked up the call I heard Priyanka's voice she was crying like hell said nothing and she kept crying soon I realized there's something wrong.

"What happen tell me?" I said as she was not stopping "Tell me naa yaar what happen" I said again Louder this time.

She tried to control her tears for a second and she only managed to say "Daddy" and then again she started crying and sobbing.

I knew something went wrong "Am coming there in half an hour" I said to her and disconnected the call as she was still crying on the phone.

I reached the lilawati hospital in a hurry and entered the private ward that her friend Sonam had told me his father was in.

Priyanka saw me and she fell on the floor near the door. Rubbing her hands in pain, she started hitting her head on the wall. She coughed, and cried like hell. I tried to pick her up. I knew what she was feeling like. I know what you feel like you lose someone very close to you, it seems like everything is ruined. All your dreams, promises, a life together- all finished.

"I want to meet him, I need him" she tried to get up and to reach her dads bed but wasn't able to. I held her. She started shouting.

"Why did this happen to me? Why...." She hit my chest hard. I held her tightly. "I am always with you" even I broke into tears too.

"Why did this happen to me? Please I want him back" she was pleading, holding my legs, putting her head on my feet.

"Please, Maddy, I never asked you for anything. Please just call him. I need him back...please" I picked her up and hugged her she continued "I won't be able to live... please. I need him" nobody was saying anything, just crying.

Her mother was hugging his body and crying.

"Why did you leave?" she cried in pain as she tore away from me and went to stand beside his dad's bed.

"You did so many things for me you faced all the difficulty that came... why did you leave? Why has this happened to me? You can't go... you can't leave like this. Say something..." she again started hitting her head against the bed and then fell into the floor and fainted.

It's very hard when you lose some one very special to you in front of your eyes and you can't do anything about it, I knew what she was going thru but I even I could do nothing about it.

Priyanka's elder brother Priyanshu came up to and me and said "you be with mummy and Priyanka, we need to take dad's body for all other procedure in the hospital and then cremation" I could see tears in his eyes which he was trying to control. "Yes" I said and moved towards Priyanka her uncle's made her sleep on the bed where his dad left the world I sat on a chair beside her bed holding her hand. She was badly hurt as she was very close to his dad; he was the only one who had fulfilled her every wish without any questions.

After a person dies cremation is an extremely important ritual for Hindus and people belonging to most of the other religion. Hindus believe it releases an individual's soul from its temporary physical body so it can be reborn. Traditionally women have not been allowed at the ceremonies because it is believed that they are emotionally not as strong as men and they might cry and cannot handle the emotional trauma associated with this act.

So as his brother said I stayed up there with Priyanka and her mother and made sure everyone had something to eat and drink there were many of her relatives as well and I recognized none of them. We left the hospital by evening Priyanka still didn't gained senses she was made sleep in her bedroom. As I was about to leave her home night at 11:00PM her mother walked towards me and said

"Beta thanks for whatever you did today for us"

I just said "Aunty don't say that I did it because you all are like a family to me"

"Could you do me a favor" her mother said wiping her tears off.

"Yes aunty for sure just say" I said keeping my car keys into the back pocket of my jeans.

"Can you stay here tonight? I don't know if Priyanka wakes up how we would make her stop crying" she said and cried again.

"Yes aunty I'll stay here, please don't cry" I said holding her hands into mine but couldn't make her stop crying. I was feeling so helpless I could do nothing to make them smile.

I stayed up there that night and as Priyanka's mother said she woke up at night and the only question she asked to me was "Where is my dad?" and I could say nothing to her and she hugged me and cried her heart out almost whole night. Death leaves a heartache no one can heal.

At morning she was slept and I was sitting beside her bed when her mom entered the room and said "Beta have tea" and handed me the cup of tea.

"Aunty I think I should leave now" I said standing up.

"No beta please stay I'll wake her up" Mrs.Verma moved ahead to wake up Priyanka.

"No aunty let her sleep I don't want her to cry again" I said stopping Mrs.Verma from waking her up.

"Ok" she said and went out of the room and I followed her.

"Bye aunty take care" I said touching her feet and then moving towards my shoes. And then I saw her mother crying again.

I moved towards her and hugged her mother and I could feel her tears all over my shoulder that made me broke into tears as well only thing I managed to say at that point was

"Aunty you have so many beautiful memories with uncle that'll bring peace during this difficult time, am so sorry for your loss, am always here for you, you have to be strong for your kids please don't cry" I said I wiped her tears. Nobody in the world could see a mother cry even thou if she is not your mother.

"Thank you beta "she said and wiped my tears off.

"Bye aunty take care and do have something" I said as I came pressed the button of the lift.

I was always worried of Priyanka she was so much attached to his father that it seems impossible for her to survive. I always called her mother up to know how everything is.

It was the last week of July when I got a call from Sonam and she informed me that Priyanka was been hospitalized due to low BP.

I took all the information from her and went to meet Priyanka that same day.

I entered the clinic of Dr. Agarwal in Andheri east he was the family doctor of Vermas

I saw her mom sitting on a chair beside Priyanka's bed.

"Oh beta, you come" aunty was surprised to see me and stood up. I touched her feet. My eyes fell on the mother who was still fighting with her tears and managed to keep a smile on her face just for her kids.

Priyanka slid up and leaned on the wall. "Think of the devil and the devil is here" she said in a lazy voice. Her words and expressions showed that she was expecting me.

I came close to her bed, "Without informing me, you've come here" I pinched her nose.

The room smelled strongly of sterile chemical sanitizer. She smiled, her face was dry but still her smile kept up the faith in everyone that she'd be better soon though I wasn't sure she was there. Aunty stood up and sat on the stool. I came sat where her mother was sitting.

"Beta, you have to take your medicines. Have something" her mother said to her holding medicines in her hand.

"Ma, I don't want to eat. I'll have after sometime," she said

"Aunty, give it to me, I'm also hungry, and we will both have some food" I took the bowl from her mother.

"You hungry you didn't have anything from morning? And who told you that am here? Must be Sonam right" she shot few question at a time.

"Madam ji zyaada sawaal jawaab nahi! Shut up and have this" I said and handed her the bowl of salad.

She took it and had some from it and then she said "How's you now are getting over her or still? Pyaar, mohabbat, ishq"

"Leave it naa" I said and took the medicines from her mother sitting beside me.

"Denial is the first sign that you dint accept it" she said and gave a tough look.

"Do I still need to show you more proof?" she added

I kept silent for a minute and thought about whatever she had said. She had said nothing wrong.

"Let me find her once" I said as that emptiness returned to my heart.

"Maddy you found her once you even had word with her and what she did she ignored you right! Don't you get it? Why are you finding ways to get yourself hurt again and again" she said angrily.

And I still kept quiet and heads down as if I have not done my homework and getting scolded from the teacher.

"I can help you" she said again.

"Help in what sense?"

"Every day, you have to come here after office. Have one cup of coffee with me and listen to whatever I say. And we will not talk about Shatabdi"

"That's interesting, but I can't promise anything. I'll think about it" I said and stood up and gave her the medicine.

"It's not a big thing, just a coffee... and don't worry, I won't allow you take advantage of me" she said as she inserted her fingers in mouth to have the medicines directly into her throat

"Moreover it's just a matter of five days" she said after finishing the glass of water.

"Five days? What after five days?" I said bit confusingly.

"I'll be gone" she said and tears rolled down her cheeks.

"Hey what happen sweetheart where are you going?" I said holding her hands.

"New Zealand" her mother said from behind.

"New Zealand?" I repeated "For how many days?" I added. As Dr.Agarwal entered the room.

"Hello uncle" Priyanka said wiping her tears off.

"You crying again beta" he said and went towards her.

Mean while Priyanka's mother held my hand and we came out the room and sat in the corridor and then she said. "Beta she'll be going New Zealand on fifth august and might not be coming back again"

"Achanak?' I said as I was confused.

"Yes beta from the day her father passed away she's been living in trauma, she gets fainted almost daily, she cries like anything, she doesn't even eat properly" her mother said as sitting next to me and holding my hands and I could see the pain in her eyes.

I know how it feels when someone you loved more than life lives you. Everything that reminds you of that person haunts you and you can't do anything about it. You only wish to be with that person even though if there are many people beside you.

"So I want her to be happy, so decided this and even she is ready for it" she added.

"That's great aunty even I was worried about her, she always talked about her dad when we use to meet, and you have done the right thing she doesn't deserve to be sad and even you" I said and we stood up.

As we came inside she was done with her checkups the doctor called Mrs. Verma in his cabin for some discussion. And we both talked for hours after that I left from there promising her to be there at her departure.

Soon the day came when my best friend was leaving India forever her flight was at 11:35PM from Mumbai airport we reached the airport at 7:00PM as the rule we needed to reach three hours prior the departure but we managed to reach almost 4.30 hours prior.

As she stepped out of the car I was busy removing her luggage from the car Priyanka came up to me and said "You'll be fine naa?" the way she said that "naa" it reminded me of Shatabdi.

"I am fine" I said.

"Promise me you'll move on, promise me you'll never cry, promise me you'll never go searching her again, just promise me" she raised her voice.

"So much promises, I'll choose only one from them" I said and laughed.

"Just Look at you Maddy, do you think I don't anything?" she said angrily.

"What?" I said.

"What life do you have? Do you even remember when did you smile in the last six months? Moreover, keep your wallet. You forget it in the car" she laughed, handling me my wallet.

"Oh shit, how did I forget my wallet? I said taking it from her.

"And I say it again please move on you deserve a much better life, you are a sweetheart" she hugged me for the last time as I kept her luggage onto the trolley. Then she moved towards her mom and I excused them.

She again came towards me and said "Give me your phone I need to inform Polly about it her number is not reachable I tried many times" as she took my cell phone and messaged my sister about her departure. They both were very good friends they both got to know each other the way me and Priyanka got in touch the social networking site "Face book".

"Toh I should leave now" she said with tears in her eyes.

"Hey why are you crying?" I said.

"I Miss my dad if he would have been here, he would have never let me go" she said while hiding her face behind the scarf.

"Those we love they walk beside us every day, unseen, unheard, but always near, still loved still missed and very dear" I said and hugged her for the last time.

And then she moved away from us. I saw her thru the mirror waving her hands to us. And showing her index finger to. As knew what she was trying to say.

But giving up your dream day by day is like watching yourself die in pain day by day nobody can understand that pain and that is why it is much painful.

Now I knew it was really over between me and Shatabdi. I wasn't the same person I was almost a year and half ago, the love for someone who would never feel the same way about me, it wasn't that I decided to stop caring about her... I just finally decided to care about myself.

Then I took a deep breath... and tried to apply the promise Priyanka asked me for...

Although I never agreed with her...

I might have erased her texts but I will never forget what she wrote. We might have stopped talking, but I will never forget her voice, we might have stopped hugging, but I will never forget how she smells. Anything we did I will never forget, you never really stop loving someone you just learn to try to live without them...

ACT SIXTEEN

The Darjeeling Affect

Suddenly I was all alone, that was the moment when I started missing my sister, I missed her a little, a little too much, a little too often, and a little more each day. Polly is a sweet, innocent and decent girl she didn't like partying much but went out for a few only with her best friends. She knew very well what she wanted from life. She was one of those girls who had never been in relationship but had numerous crushes starting from Salman Khan to Ranbir Kapoor. Quite a few boys were attracted to her but she never responded to any of them.

I can blindly say that she'll be the best home maker because she knows exactly what she wants and how to go about it. You cannot lie in front of her because she'll know with your looks that you are hiding stuff in my case she got to know it on phone every time I tried to hide something from her. She'll give you the best direct and honest answers which are hard to accept but still are true. I fight with her argue with her yet love her the most.

I decided to be there with my sister on my birthday so I booked the ticket to Delhi of 29th august.

I remember when I once visited her during her first year of college she introduced me to one of her friend named Dipika Verma she was her senior from 'Darjeeling', doing a Dietetics course at the amity university. I didn't noticed her much then but when I came home I always use to ask Polly about Dipika repeatedly no I wouldn't say I fell in love with her then. I wouldn't say I felt attracted to her. But I felt something deep inside, strong enough for my heart to say "hey you have to talk to this girl at least once in your life"

I reached Delhi's Indira Gandhi Airport at morning Irrespective of what time of the day it is. Delhi always has a fresh look about it and the credit for this goes to Delhi girls.

How do they manage to put on so much make up? It's so early morning and here they are, complete with mascara, lip gloss and eye liner, wearing the latest collection of fashionable, branded kurtis, I thought.

My eyes fell upon a group of pretty girls who were waiting for the metro. I realized that the glow on their faces and their confidence was what made Indian women so special. These qualities really set them apart and made a great case for Indian beauty being the best in the world.

Standing there I remembered those days with Shatabdi when I used to wait for her. Nothing changed in the last two years… if anything had changed; it was me and my circumstances.

I took metro from Airport metro station to New Delhi metro station and then another metro to Jahangirpuri. I followed the instruction as given by my cousin brother Alok as it was the first time I was traveling in Delhi metro.

The best thing about the metro was you got to know which the upcoming station is and which side the door's going to get opened as after Adarsh nagar metro station the announcement echoed in the metro.

"Agla station Jahangirpuri darwaze bayein or khulenge"

"Next station Jahangirpuri doors will open on the left"

I Came out of Jahangirpuri metro station and he was there to pick me up. We came to the parking area and got onto the bike for a mini ride as we reached his room where he lived in 10 minutes. Room or should it was a matchbox I wonder how he lived there it was so congested but whatever it was it was the place where I had to be for the next two days.

It was 12'o clock at night my phone vibrated as I received some birthday wishes messages from some old and new friends. The only message I was waiting was the message I didn't received. I found it funny that there was a point in time where we were together and I literally did everything for her and now she doesn't even text me to see if I'm okay. And if I did she didn't bothered replying, it's just weird how time changes things.

Next morning Polly and I decide to meet at the Connaught place and as I was new in Delhi I got the directions from her., I needed to take a metro from Jahangirpuri and get down at Rajiv Chowk metro station.

And I did as she said. I was waiting near the escalator at the Rajiv Chowk gate no.1 and wondered If we were supposed to meet at Connaught place why did she said me to get down at Rajiv Chowk confusingly I thought.

"Bhaiyya" she shouted from back. And there she was holding a cake in her right hand and her bag and other little stuff in the other hand. It was good to see a familiar face in thousand of unknown people in an unknown city. I felt relaxed I forget all my worries as it is said 'someone's goodbye could crush your heart but someone's hello could patch it back together' and in my case that someone was my little sister Polly.

"Hey betu how are you?" I said and moved forward to give her a hug.

"Ye pakdo pehle" she said passing the cake from her right hand to mine and then she added "Happy Birthday" and hugged me and I hugged her back.

"Thank you! Now first tell me we were suppose to meet at Connaught place then why you said me to get down here" I asked her as I was confused from the time I got down at the Rajiv Chowk metro station.

"You are an idiot you know that, come I'll show you something" she said as we walked out of the metro station and she said again "Look at this" she showed me the place which I always watched in films or papers it was that famous white colored heritage like structures.

"Oh then why the station is called Rajiv Chowk instead of Connaught place?" I questioned.

"You need to ask that to the Delhi government" she said and we laughed and then we moved towards the CCD at Connaught place we got seated there and she went to get knife not to cut my head off but the cake she got for me from her university and it looked delicious.

"This is for you" she handed me some boxes wrapped in gift papers and it took me less than five minutes to unwrap it, and it was two wonderful T-Shirt which became my favorite as soon as I saw them.

"I loved it" I said and gave her the biggest piece of the cake.

After cutting the cake and having some coffee we decided to have something as we both were hungry all we did from the time we met was talk, talk and talk. We roamed all around the CP but we didn't manage to get any restaurant empty to be seated and have something peacefully. So we decided to have our lunch at the McDonalds and we moved in we had some burgers French fries and float coke although these cannot be called as lunch but still we got some energy for the rest of the day.

We talked about everything, about our family, about Shatabdi, about Priyanka, about her studies, about my relationship with dad, and about that gorgeous girl Dipika as well. I believed the real power of a man is in the size of the smile of the women sitting next to him as I looked my sister I felt like so powerful as I made her smiled all the time. And then I decided to visit her next day at her university as she only managed to get a one day out pass.

Heading back towards the Rajiv Chowk station in the evening a kid came up to us and begun to ask for the money I always wondered why can't their parents send them to government school which offers free education to all the children below poverty line in India.

"Cake khayega" I asked to little boy and he nodded.

"Kitne log ho tum log" I asked and he said "Panch"

"oh ye lo" I said and handed him the box of the cake and added "sab milke khaana akele mat khaa lena sab"

He took the box in an instance and ran with his friends to enjoy my birthday those smile on their little face was priceless. I read somewhere once 'If you find someone without a smile give, them one of yours' and so do I did although there was nothing much to smile about in my life.

We took the metro from Rajiv Chowk again and then got down at the Iffco Chowk metro station and then a cab from there to the Amity University. I dropped her at the gate and promised to be there tomorrow and I returned back to the matchbox.

Next day morning I repeated the same travelling mode as Polly suggested me the last night, a metro from Jahangirpuri to Iffco Chowk and then a cab from Iffco Chowk to Amity University. Her university was located bit inside from the Delhi-Jaipur highway near the small Rocky Mountains which gave university a beautiful look in its own way I wished if I could live that hostel life for once.

I reached the university morning near about 11 or 12 and waited for Polly outside the girl's hostel and there she came in next minutes wearing a blue denim shirt and black jeans we made our way to grab a seat in CCD located inside the campus just in front of the girl's hostel

"Coffee?" I asked Polly as we entered the CCD.

"Nope! I'll have ice tea" she responded.

"Okay you have seat I'll order it" I said and moved towards the counter "One medium cappuccino and one ice tea" I said to the guy sitting at the counter. Coffee was always like a drug, a warm delicious drug for me.

"Here you are" I said as I came back to the seat where Polly was sitting.

"So Bhaiyya, kisne kisne wish kiya kal" she said as she kept her phone on to the table.

"Everyone except Dipika" I said and laughed.

"Ha Ha very funny" she said. Polly always knew I had feelings for Dipika as I always use to talk about her likes and dislikes, how she is and other stuff. And on the other hand I just felt something inside it wasn't love but yes slowly-slowly I was getting attracted to her without even knowing her. Maybe because I was living a committed relationship from the past 10 years and suddenly I was single.

It was around 4PM time passed so rapidly when we both siblings where together.

"Should I call her here?" Polly said looking at her phone.

"Who Dipika? I murmured.

"Yes! She just messaged me that she finished her class and coming this side" Polly added.

"No No No NO" I said almost five times to make sure she heard it.

"Why NO! You like her, don't you?" she raised her eyebrows.

"Yes I do but I can't talk to her" I said as I started feeling nervous as if I am about to face IIT entrance exam paper.

"I don't know anything she is standing outside am taking her in" she stood up and went outside.

A moment later...

I could only see Dipika walking towards me with her friend mini and my sister Polly, as if I had blinders on. She

159

was looking brighter that the sun. This isn't the movies, I remember telling myself, but why had the people sitting next to our table frozen in place and why did time slow down. I could see her smile from far. It was shy yet pretty, confident yet tragic, she resembled the girl I saw in my dreams, beautiful and complex, the world seemed like it would end every time she blinked, hiding her hazel eyes.

She reminded me of a poem from Shakespeare, magical and complex, each feature of her hiding a different story, her prettiness was epic and rich, just like nobody else in the world could match her.

She was not that tall, maybe five-feet-one, but those eyes, man, those eyes. My heart thumped as she had seat in front of me, my breaths were heavy and deliberate, and I trembled. There was certain happiness in her prettiness, like she would smile and everything in the world would be okay.

"HI! Belated Happy Birthday" Dipika said.

Some say there is an exact moment when you fall in love. I didn't know if it was before from the past 2 year, but I do now, this was it. When Dipika Verma said that line, my heart whispered "She's the One". The world turned in slow motion. I noticed her delicate eyebrows. When she spoke they moved slightly. They had the perfect length, thickness and width, she would win a "best eyebrows" competition there itself, I didn't even wanted to blink at that time; I just didn't wanted to miss a second of her cuteness.

"Thank You" I said and I went blank as if I am in a coma. The moment when Polly said she is taking her in I rehearsed few lines so that I could manage to talk to her but still my all efforts got into a vain and only thing I managed to say was "Thank you" such a dumb guy you are Maddy I was thinking In my mind as Polly and Dipika where talking something about Sarojni nagar.

"Bye" Dipika said as she stood up and yet again like an idiot I said "Bye".

First impression is the last impression and I have ruined my first impression I said in mind I wish I could undo that. And meet her once again for the first time to tell her how gorgeous she is, I just had a glimpse of her eyes but I could see my world in it. I lost in my thoughts.

"Thank You! Hahaha" Polly said and laughed like a devil as she imitated the way I said 'Thank you' to Dipika.

"Oh shut up! I was confused yaar" I said and took a sip of coffee.

"Hahaha... You were sounding like a girl brother" she tried to control her laughter.

"Anything, just anything" I said and tried to look away as I was embarrassed my sister was making fun of me what would Dipika be thinking now shit I man I ruined it I thought and recollected the way I reacted in front of her.

"Koi baat nai Bhai, there's always a second time" she said as she noticed I was bit upset about that.

"Hmm! I hope so, chalo now I should leave it takes almost 2hours to reach Jahangirpuri from your university" I said and kept the cup of coffee on the table.

And she came till the gate to drop me we hugged and waved each other a goodbye. I feel blessed to have a sister like her she is laws like a best friend you can't get rid of. I knew whatever I do she'll still be there. There is no better friend than a sister and there is no better sister than she is.

Next day I flew back to Mumbai and since then my calls to Polly was tripled over the last week because I wanted to hear Dipika's voice in the background somewhere. It just kept ringing in my head since that day and no matter what I did, it stayed there. It didn't take long for Polly to put two and two together.

"Bhaiyya, one more word about her and we will never talk again," she said.

It was millionth time that day that I had picked her name up in a conversation. But still I talked and talked about her again and again. It had been almost more than two months and I had not been able to push the thought of her out of my mind. I kept day dreaming about her, constructed fake dates with her, where I would just sit and she tell everything about her and anything she wants to speak.

I was now a Facebook friend of Dipika courtesy Polly. Whenever I had a word with Polly I always talked about Dipika.

I gathered some courage to talk to Dipika on Facebook it's easy to talk to the same person thru a social media website whom you are afraid to talk as a person at least in my case though.

Few days later she even texted me on my number trying to play a prank on me as a wrong number. I was trapped in her prank for a minute but as soon as I saw her display picture on Whatsapp I knew it was she. I was so happy at least she bothered to text me, we chatted about random stuff until she was sleepy.

Could I have been more humorous, just to impress her further? Was the chat perfect or not? Was my way of chatting good? Would Dipika be thinking about the conversation too? I questioned myself. I predictably, didn't want to discuss this pleasant moment with others. Alone in my home, I was smiling at nobody in particular, and there was different sort of feeling within me. "Why are you so excited and frenzied to talk to her again? Then I realized I was such a foolish guy but true with my thoughts. I looked at the mirror, which always listened me, "relax dude. There is always a tomorrow".

Form the next day I started greeting her by a "Good Morning" and a "Good night" message's and she responded the same.

But few days later she stopped responding to messages, every day I felt like messaging her at least to know the reason why she wasn't responding to my messages but I couldn't talk to her because she didn't replied me the previous time and I didn't wanted to annoy her by starting another conversation with her. It's like I was dying to talk her but I knew she don't want to talk to me. So I stopped bothering her.

Few weeks later I was at Rocky's place I just wanted to forget everything

I went to the kitchen to get knife, I had brought some apples for both of us... "Hey, did u had a word with her again" rocky said standing behind me with a beer in his hand and an apple in another one, weird combination well that's what he is... 'Weird'

Busy finding the knife, I answered "with whom," I knew exactly he was talking about Dipika...

"C'mon don't act like a saint" he said he also knew that I was avoiding his question... "Shall I ask you something" he continued. .

Having some idea of what he was about to ask, I laughed a bit and said, "Dude, enjoy the beer and give me one"

I continued hunting for the knife. Rocky's eyes were still on me.

Trying to steer rocky away from the topic that was on his mind, I spoke again. "Kal office kab hai tera?"

"Do you love her?" he asked with a big bite of the apple. He was looking intently at me...

"Are you crazy? There is no such thing!" I exclaimed as I found the knife under the gas stove." Oh, here it is. Come, let's go out and have Steve jobs product peacefully" I winked and laughed at my own joke.

"Why are you avoiding my question Maddy?" Rocky persisted the voices from the bedroom had suddenly become louder. Vijay has raised the music's volume to a high peach...

"Come on, yaar! Paagal hai kya?" I said facing the kitchen door. Rocky was behind me.

"You like her or not?" he repeated.

I turned towards him and took a deep breath. "You know my past very well, bro. "I was going to continue but rocky cut me mid speech...

"Yes, very well, but it doesn't mean you can't live your life again" Rocky's voice was louder this time and having a big gulp of beer.

I wasn't left with much to say. Deep inside even I knew that I liked Dipika 'A LOT" I stood still, vaguely looking at the knife which I was holding in my hand.

"Maddy, it's been a long time now. Think about your future, get yourself a life" rocky said keeping his right hand on my shoulder, as he made an attempt to convince me, what I already know!

Rocky knew everything about me; he was like a brother to me. I know he was absolutely justified in saying these things to me, but I wasn't wrong either. I knew I wanted a change, but getting another girl wasn't the change. I wanted to experience a change in terms of my daily life, my surroundings, the culture and the people I interacted with. Of course I found Dipika to be a nice and beautiful girl, it was exciting for me to see her but I never imagined myself falling in love with her but I was already fallen.

Not that I never thought that way, but whenever I thought of it, I couldn't give myself an honest answer, I would tell myself to simply leave it all up to destiny.

His words didn't register in my mind. I stood quietly to let him finish speaking what his heart felt. Alcohol makes people speak from their hearts. Rocky was now speaking from his.

"Bro I know you love her u just need to tell her" rocky added.

"It won't matter to her, aur waise bhi Polly told me she likes a guy in her university I hope even the guy falls for her, Dipika is such a cute girl" I said with a smile.

"Oh don't give me that bullshit, if you don't say her I'll message her on my own, how can she just ignore the effort of a person who was trying to keep in touch, people get tired, it's not all times that they hold on" rocky said raising his eyebrows.

"Maybe she is not interested in me and I'll kick your ass very badly if you dare to message her the choice is yours" I replied in an instance.

"What the fuck, dude there's always going to be that girl who is prettier than her, she just need to find the one guy

ACT SEVENTEEN

The Present

I saw Shatabdi once after two years have passed since we spoke. I avoided that side of town to make sure I don't see her, but today I just ran into her office and stood in the corridors, waiting for her office to end; I stood far away and avoided any contact. I watched her come out of office, only to disappear into the crowd, I wanted to sit and just watch her. My heart still aches for my lost love.

In the last 2 years, there hasn't been a moment when I didn't thought about Shatabdi. I can't understand why thinking about her always makes me cry. I'm a strong man, I have always told myself. Now when she's gone, I realize that she was my strength. I wish I could have been the person who could keep her happy. I wish I could touch her heart again as I did once upon a time. I wish she had never gone. I wish she was here. I wish she loved me. I wish all my wishes come true. You come true. "WE COME TRUE" sometimes you just have to pretend that you are happy just to stop everyone from asking what happened.

I had zero ability to get over her. I couldn't believe a girl who had left me two years ago had such a grip on me. She was the first girl I had played, walked, eaten, talked, studied and had fun with. I had peeked into silent Shatabdi more than anyone else, or so I thought. How could I forget? Every time I say I won't remember her, I end up remembering her. This time I would stick to my words. I'm a man of my words: I should live up to my image. When she was there, I could easily deny the fact that I love her, sometimes just to play around with her, sometimes just to hurt her, but now when she is gone, I can't deny it. Not even once. I Loved Her. More than I ever realized I could. Her happiness, her smile when she was standing on the other side of the road, her laugh, her walk, her fingers, her smell, her silky hair, her toes, her small feet.

I wish. I wish many things. Some realistic, some not and some, just needful.

She left me. But still, she was left in me.

She has left me, by her own choice – a choice which I respect, a choice which I understand and a choice that has drawn me closer to her. I don't expect her to come back. I do wish, however. I wish a lot. I wish that some things didn't happen. I wish I hadn't said something's. I wish I was not in love. I wish my life were as dreamlike as it was on the first day. I wish she wasn't there. I wish . . . oh why do I wish?

Now it was like whenever I see a couple holding hands, or just plainly sitting together I look away it's not that I hate seeing lovers but because it reminds me of a question nobody can answer. 'Where's Mine?' Love can be beautiful but sometimes cupids bow and arrow can take very misdirected aim. In my case the cupid aimed me two times but didn't bother to aim the other one... Once it lasted for almost ten years and in another one I was taken for granted because she knew I had feelings for her.

They say there is a reason for everything I still could not recollect any of the reasons why I and Shatabdi fall apart, and then falling in love again with a girl who didn't even know about it. In the past two years I experienced everything which doesn't really happen in someone's lifetime. I never really thought I will turned into someone's best friend, Priyanka is miles away from me but still we are connected as we were previously and still remain the best friend as always. Dipika is now just a Facebook friend who just sometime likes my posts and I still like her as I ever did since the time I saw her in Café Coffee Day. Now I have one girl who made my existence meaningful and that's my lovely sister Polly, she is my everything.

There's nothing called true or fake love; it's all about how we look at it, how we treat it and what we make of it. As I begin to complete my love story I have many thoughts in my mind. Whether this story would end. What does it mean when I say an end? Does it need an end?

Or just a new beginning...

Printed in the United States
By Bookmasters